PRAISE FOR
HOW TO BE

"Snow fell outside my dark study as I read these exquisitely
simple letters by computer light. I was a blissed-out fly on
their writing desks as I buzzed back and forth between these
wise words exchanged between a married woman and a
monk. In the end, I was overjoyed for having spent hours
in their good company. Their friendship saturated me with
comfort and calm. So many good words made me happy,
especially 'I know you and you know me. But wait. I hardly
know myself—at least not, as yet, in the totality of what I will
be. The little letters we write, the casual contacts we make in
life, the fragments of acquaintance, the relationships, broken
or made whole, are just the beginning. Each is a small seed of
what can develop in eternity. None of it is ever lost. Nothing is
ever lost.' Oh, thank you both for including me."

—JON MONTALDO, editor of *The Intimate
Merton* (with Brother Patrick Hart)

"These letters remind us that the monastic life is a gift to the
world. The prayers and teachings of monks and nuns are here
to help make contemplatives of all of us, regardless of where
we live."

—JON M. SWEENEY, coauthor of *Meister Eckhart's Book of
the Heart;* translator of *Francis of Assisi in His Own Words*

"This small book brought me joy and solace at a difficult time—what more may I say? Such a pleasure to read the correspondence of two thoughtful, perceptive people about what really matters. This small book demonstrates again that letters are among our most important literary forms."

—FENTON JOHNSON, author of *At the Center of All Beauty*

"This book is 'a small taste of eternity' as Judith and Br. Paul invite us into stories of ancient wisdom lived in contemporary contexts. Modeled through letter writing and spiritual friendship, they tackle some of the biggest questions: change and stability, humility and purpose, time and eternity, life and the afterlife. This book preserves ageless monastic wisdom as monasticism itself is evolving before our eyes. People of all spiritual backgrounds and across generations will find insight on how to live through challenging times, personally and societally, in these pages."

—KATIE GORDON, cofounder of Nuns and Nones
and staff member of Monasteries of the Heart

HOW
TO BE

*A Monk and a Journalist
Reflect on Living & Dying,
Purpose & Prayer,
Forgiveness & Friendship*

JUDITH VALENTE
PAUL QUENON, OCSO

Foreword by Kathleen Norris

HAMPTON ROADS

Copyright © 2021
by Judith Valente and Paul Quenon
Foreword copyright © 2021 by Kathleen Norris

Cover design by Kathryn Sky-Peck
Cover photograph *Avenue* © Sara Hayward/Bridgeman Images
Interior by Maureen Forys, Happenstance Type-O-Rama
Typeset in Sabon and Centaur

Hampton Roads Publishing Company, Inc.
Charlottesville, VA 22906
Distributed by Red Wheel/Weiser, LLC

Sign up for our newsletter and special offers by going to
www.redwheelweiser.com/newsletter.

ISBN: 978-1-64297-034-0

Library of Congress Cataloging-in-Publication Data available upon request.

Printed in the United States of America
IBI

10 9 8 7 6 5 4 3 2 1

For my husband,
Charles Reynard,
and for the monks of
the Abbey of Gethsemani—
past, present, and future.

TABLE OF CONTENTS

FOREWORD

This book of correspondence is a refreshment, a reminder that although "interconnectivity" has become a buzzword, and technology allows us to contact one another in a dazzling variety of new ways, something vital is missing. Emails travel around the world in seconds, but in gaining efficiency and speed, we risk losing the ability to listen. We long for deeper communion with others, and this book shows us one way to find it.

How to Be introduces us to Judith Valente, a married woman, a journalist and retreat leader with a hectic schedule, and Brother Paul Quenon, a celibate and a contemplative Cistercian monk of the Abbey of Gethsemani. We all benefit from the decision they made to deepen their relationship by means of letters. Br. Paul's helpful comment about the difference between an email message and correspondence is borne out in etymology. The word "message" is related to "mission" and implies using words to advance an agenda. The word "correspondence," by comparison, is derived from "engagement," suggesting something deeper, a pledge to be open and honest with another person. In corresponding with a friend, we have no agenda other than fostering friendship.

That's inspiring, but the reader might wonder about the value of paying attention to the ramblings of two people, as interesting as they are. Reading their letters could seem as meaningless as hearing another person's dreams. But the subjects these two touch on are universal. We all deal with illness and death, grief and loss, work, play, and the use of our time, and the musings in these letters can help us determine our own path through the glorious mess called life.

Like Judith, most of us know what it's like to be so consumed by work that we lose sleep over it. We fret over being so overloaded and distracted that at the end of the day we feel it's all been wasted time. But few of us hear the wisdom of Br. Paul's response to her lament: that a good way to get over the feeling that you're wasting your time is to waste more of it. He suggests that she intentionally slow down and look around her to see what's really there. How liberating to embrace his Zen-like wisdom, that the purpose of life is that it doesn't need a purpose: the purpose of life is life.

It's good to hear two thoughtful people reflecting on their lived experience. Judith, a self-described "over-achiever," is often anxious and Paul is more calm, reflecting on the fruits of a monastic life structured so as to foster contemplation. Both are modern people, well aware of the uneasiness that pervades our culture. But Paul reminds is that it's all right to admit that we don't always know what to hope for. If we don't understand what's happening to and around us, maybe that's how God wants it. Citing a comment by his mentor Thomas

Merton that Jesus will always seek out the most lowly crib, he adds that the holy is often found in the places we are most reluctant to look.

Many of us can identify with Judith's difficulty in devoting time to pray, let alone praying attentively, and with Br. Paul's admission that he tends to fall asleep when he's meditating. Fortunately their views on spirituality and religion are not sectarian, and both reflect on experiences with people of other faiths. Paul offers an indelible image of Buddhist monks playing soccer with children outside Merton's hermitage; Judith discusses her study of meditation with a Tibetan Lama. As Christians, both ponder their experience of receiving the eucharist at Mass. Judith speaks of the wonder of carrying the body of Christ within her; Paul says it makes him realize that every Christian is a reincarnation of Christ.

One thing that connects these two disparate people is poetry, and it's delightful to see the way they share their own poems as well as the work of others who have inspired them: Emily Dickinson, Walt Whitman, and a contemporary, Mary Oliver. Poets do not shy away from difficult subjects, and the reflections on suffering and death in these letters have been especially helpful to me. Judith recalls that a man she'd interviewed for a *Wall Street Journal* article told her, as he neared death, that "the line between life and death is thinner than you think." A Benedictine monastery is a thin place by design, as each monk lives with Benedict's admonition in his Rule for monks, to "keep death daily before your eyes."

Judith says she's always struggled with the Christian notion of death as being "born to eternal life, as lovely as that sounds." And Paul admits that he rarely thinks about heaven, but finds "much of the Resurrection in our love of the world and of the beauty that nature presents. In loving nature, in loving the world, we love something larger than ourselves, and we are made larger by that loving."

This book is a generous invitation to a conversation, a word with special meaning for Benedictines. One of the vows they make is to *conversatio morum,* loosely translated as "conversion of life." The word "conversation" is rooted in a word meaning to turn, to change, to be versatile rather than rigid. And the joy of conversation in that sense enriches these letters. In discussing the effects of the pandemic, for example, Judith says that the enforced isolation made her deeply grateful to see her mail carrier every day, and allowed her to engage in cooking as a meditative practice. Paul reminds us that "love starts at home," and with people spending more time with their families the pandemic might be seen as a challenge to develop more compassion and empathy.

This book has given me a challenge: I now want to think of someone, a friend living close by or far away, who would be willing to engage in the kind of meandering but deeply meaningful correspondence contained in this book.

—Kathleen Norris,
author of *The Cloister Walk*

INTRODUCTION:
Seeds of a Friendship

The first time I climbed a tree I was an adult. My climbing partner was a sixty-nine-year-old Trappist monk named Brother Paul Quenon.

Brother Paul cheered me on as I lumbered haltingly up the limbs of a magnolia on the grounds of the Abbey of Gethsemani, located outside of Louisville, Kentucky. Tree-climbing was not the only challenge he gave me. He urged me to walk backward occasionally to see a familiar place from a fresh perspective. He recommended that, once in a while, I stroll barefoot outside to "regain the intelligence" of my feet. From Brother Paul, I learned that contemplation—the calm, recollected, prayerful interior that monks work years to attain and many of us non-monks yearn to experience—is "just a big fat word for gratitude."

Over the years, I had many chances to spend time with Brother Paul. He entered monastic life at the age of seventeen and has practiced a life of contemplation for more than sixty years. Men and women with that depth of monastic experience will, like an endangered species, likely no longer exist within a few years. They are becoming extinct. Each time I visit Gethsemani, there are fewer monks than before. Sometimes new faces arrive, but they are mostly middle-aged men, widowed or divorced, who carry experience from business and the professions. By my next visit, they are usually gone. This pattern of subtraction is unfolding in monasteries across the world. As a result, we are losing the spiritual depth that only those who have spent a lifetime focused on seeking God can pass on to us.

This book aims to preserve some of that wisdom before it fades forever, through the letters Brother Paul and I have exchanged over a period of several years. These letters encompass practical matters, like knowing when to leave a job or how to deal with loss, and learning to balance doing with being. They delve into theological concerns in ways that are at once personal and universal. In them, you will find reflections on topics like prayer, meditation, the Resurrection, the Eucharist, and the future of the Church. The letters don't offer pat answers, neatly wrapped and tied with a bow. Rather, they suggest what may be the right questions for spiritual seekers to ask.

In some ways, this epistolary approach resembles the efforts of early Christian pilgrims, who sought out monks and monastic sisters living in the Egyptian desert hoping to gain "a word" from them. The insights into the inner life that Brother Paul shares in his letters are similar. They are "a word" to help those of us in the secular world navigate the monastic values of listening, community, hospitality, humility, simplicity, and prayer within the crucible of daily life.

We know from the early records of the desert dwellers and from correspondence from the past what monks in previous centuries thought, felt, and found of concern. As Brother Paul writes in one of his letters: "I fear such history of our own time is destined to be lost. Where will any of that be found?" But shouldn't we know as much about modern monks as we do about those who lived in the Middle Ages?

I first met Brother Paul in 2008 on a reporting assignment for PBS-TV. The occasion was the 40th anniversary of the death of the great spiritual teacher Thomas Merton. The Abbey of Gethsemani is where Merton prayed, worked, taught, and wrote, and where he grappled with his own inner struggles for twenty-seven years. When Brother Paul entered the community in 1959, Merton, known to his confrères as Father Louis, was the novice director responsible for educating new monks. He was also Brother Paul's spiritual director.

Brother Paul was assigned to accompany our PBS crew. He showed us the cramped, rundown shed that Merton named "St. Anne's," where he spent a few hours each week as a part-time hermit and worked on one of his best-known books, *Thoughts in Solitude*. We visited the austere cinder-block hermitage where Merton lived alone in the woods for the final three years of his life. We viewed his monk's cowl, his priestly chasuble, and his typewriter and eyeglasses, which are now housed at the Merton Center at Bellarmine University. These few personal possessions belonged to a man who was arguably the world's most famous modern monk.

As for Merton and for so many who passed through the abbey before me, little did I know that my first visit to Gethsemani would be a life-changing experience. During my interview with him, I asked Brother Paul about the purpose of the Trappist life in the modern world. I have never forgotten his response. The purpose of the monastic life in the modern world is "to show you don't need a purpose," he said. "The purpose of life is life. You're to live your life." This was a liberating revelation for an over-achieving, chronically stressed workaholic like myself.

Merton, an accomplished poet and ardent journal writer, had encouraged Brother Paul to write. At the time we met, Brother Paul was working on his fourth book of poems; he has since written five more. He told me on that first encounter that he writes a three-line poem, a Japanese haiku, as part of his daily meditation practice. As my own second poetry collection was about to be published, and as I was becoming increasingly drawn to the quiet rhythms and meditative practices of monastic life, I boldly asked Brother Paul if we could begin a haiku exchange.

Brother Paul and I pursued this exchange for more than three years, sharing our haiku with a Protestant minister and Zen practitioner named Michael Bever as well. Eventually, we collected ninety-nine of these poems (reflecting the ninety-nine names for God) and paired each of them with short reflections. They became the basis of our 2013 book, *The Art of Pausing: Meditations for the Overworked and Overwhelmed*. The letters you find in this book provide a kind of natural progression from our meditations in *The Art of Pausing*.

Why letters? I first considered spending time in person with Brother Paul and recording our conversations. That posed some difficulties, however. I am a married woman with a hectic writing and speaking schedule. The amount of time a Trappist monk is free to spend with guests is also limited. Brother Paul suggested an alternative—that we "meet" through correspondence, an idea that appealed to our shared writer's sensibility. Letters are the remnants we leave to mark important episodes in our lives. We hold on to them like heirlooms. We introduce ourselves, confide our hopes, confess our errors, offer our thanks, and say goodbye in letters. Letters comprise a literary hybrid. They are like mini private diaries that we share.

Brother Paul set a high bar for us. He wanted our correspondence to show "what we are thinking, how we are feeling, what is of immediate concern, and what we cherish in our relationship." We would go where the Spirit led us, as Brother Paul put it, "to fancy or to foundational truth." I hope you will find both fancy and foundational truth in our correspondence.

There is a long tradition of letter writing among spiritual teachers. Christianity likely would not have spread as quickly as it did without the epistles of St. Paul or the letters of Peter and James. The Book of Revelation can be viewed as one long letter from the apostle John to believers. St. John Cassian, one of the world's first roving reporters, kept records of conversations he shared with the early monks of the Egyptian desert. Through letters, we gain insight into the spiritual lessons and struggles of St. Bernard of Clairvaux, St. Thérèse of Lisieux, St. Augustine, St. Teresa of Avila, and St. John of the Cross, to name a few. By the time he died in 1968 at the age of fifty-three, Merton had written more than 20,000 letters to poets, novelists, political figures, religious leaders, and a host of other correspondents. The list of avid letter-writers goes on.

Brother Paul and I both had a sense that we would be more frank in writing to one another than we would be talking eye-to-eye, face-to-face. I believe you will find that to be the case. We decided early on to let our topics emerge organically out of whatever was happening in our lives. The letters given here are not ordered chronologically, but rather by theme. When we began writing, I was considering a major transition, deciding whether to leave my work in daily journalism. As we reflected on themes like mystery, poetry, purpose, and calling, the unexpected took on a leading role. Little did we know that, in the course of our correspondence, the COVID-19 pandemic would transform American life, I would face a major health challenge, and a racial reckoning would envelop the country. When monasteries and churches were forced to close their doors because of the pandemic, our letter writing became an even stronger spiritual lifeline.

Writing in long hand is nearly a lost art in the computer age, and both Brother Paul and I have a romantic attachment to handwritten letters. Although we considered writing to each other by hand, however, in the end, we decided to type our letters on the computer and send them as email attachments. If you could see my erratic scrawl and Brother Paul's miniscule, eye-squinting script, you'd understand why we decided to spare each other the headaches and second-guessing that were bound to occur. You won't find teardrops, coffee stains, food marks, cross-outs, or do-overs on these pages. You will find two friends sorting through their vulnerabilities, bewilderments, and uncertainties in a search for unvarnished truth.

The result is a dialogue between people stuttering to articulate life's universal questions from within highly diverse contexts and from very different perspectives. Brother Paul writes as a monk steeped in silence and the ancient prayer practices of monastic life. I write as a married professional woman striving to bring a sense of prayer and contemplation to my scattered secular life. We hope our readers will see pieces of the narrative of their own lives in our struggles and find guidance for their journey.

We don't strive in these missives to offer facile solutions or shortcuts to the lifelong struggle to deepen the interior life. Rather, taking the advice that Rainer Maria Rilke once gave to a young poet, we try to live the questions. If we reach a conclusion, it is probably because we stumbled onto it, rather than that we walked confidently into the light.

Because of the many months that Brother Paul and I were separated during the pandemic, I cherish my memories of the times we were able to be together even more. I long to return with him to one of our favorite talking spots, beneath a massive gingko tree near the abbey's entrance. I look forward to the day when we can once again take long, lingering walks across the monastery's fields, stopping long enough to sit on a rock near a pond and watch the sun descend—always mindful of making it back to the abbey in time for Vespers.

On these visits, Brother Paul occasionally challenged this city girl to jump on top of a hay roll. He could make it to the top in a single bound, then stand quite still there, towering above me like a monarch surveying his lands. Despite repeated attempts, I could never jump as high as he could. Perhaps that is a metaphor. I will never catch up to him in wisdom or in depth. Perhaps these failed attempts were another of his lessons to me—a lesson in humility.

Humility is the active ingredient that makes any letter memorable. I hope you will find it in good measure in these missives. Brother Paul and I began as writing colleagues. We became spiritual companions on a journey, and ultimately—most importantly—the best of friends.

The monks at Gethsemani had a tradition, now no longer is use, whereby they opened each conversation with the word *Benedicite*—"Bless me." The traditional reply was: *Dominus te benedicat*—"May the Lord bless you." As you embark on this journey in letters, Brother Paul and I ask for your blessing. To all who read our words, *Dominus te benedicat*.

Judith Valente
Normal, Illinois

LETTER WRITING

Dear Judith,

I am glad we agreed on a written correspondence as a suitable means of exchanging ideas. When Emily Dickinson wrote "a Letter is a joy of Earth," I think she was talking mostly of the joy of receiving a letter. But there is joy also in bringing pleasure to another with the surprise visit of a letter. In recent years, I have missed the challenge and practice of settling down to write a real letter.

I write and receive many emails, and they can be a delight, but they are mainly messages. By force of circumstance, when I first entered the monastery at the age of seventeen, I learned to write real letters—the kind you sit and mull over. The rules then were very restrictive. You could only receive letters four times a year: on Christmas, Easter, the Feast of the Assumption (August 15), and All Saints Day (November 1). Letters that arrived in between those times were saved up and delivered in a bundle on one of those holy days. It was a good practice to anticipate the letter days, to preview my thoughts before sitting down to put them into words. Words have their own peculiar dynamics, and the result can be for worse or for better. Because of the restrictions on our correspondence, any letter I received was cherished—even a boring one.

We could respond with only two letters and we had only a two-week period in which to do it. Given those circumstances, I took any letter I wrote pretty seriously, or tried to. At one point, I got permission to write more than two because my older siblings were scattered across several states. My bother Bob started calling my letters "The Epistles of St. Paul." That's when I slacked off on trying so hard to come off as pious or holy.

I could always count on letters from Mother and my older sister Carolyn. My twin sister, Eileen, was disinclined to write and I resented that. When she came for my first family visit, she wondered why I did not talk to her. I was getting back. It is appalling to me now to think of how I acted. Already I was taking letters too seriously.

My three older brothers did not write either. They left that job to their wives while they carried on with their developing careers. Because of that, I missed the opportunity to get to know them better. Still, it was great to write to their wives, who had more time, and I got to know each of them more deeply that way. I still have some of those letters after sixty years. To reread them is like parachuting into another lifetime. I hesitate to dredge up that many feelings, however, so they sit gathering dust.

At that developing age, I assumed letter writing was mainly an activity for women rather than men. I knew my Novice Master, Father Louis (Thomas Merton), wrote many letters, but he was an obvious exception. Over the years, I have developed many male friendships. It is great when I am with these friends, but we hardly ever write. The only exceptions are the men I know who are writers, like the young poet Dave Harrity. After Dave and I promised to correspond in long hand, I enjoyed sitting outside with a pad on the arm of my lawn chair, filling out ledger lines while the Spirit led me where it will. There is a special kind of knowing of words that comes through the hand as it writes. That too is "a joy of earth."

Today, our former restrictions on letters have been lifted. Even Trappists now have email and can send and receive messages at any time. Oddly, I find I communicate with my family less than ever. Maybe the difficulty of writing provided an incentive that is no longer there.

Ironically, letters were more common in those periods of history when it was more difficult to obtain writing materials and send and receive correspondence. The Middle Ages marked a golden era of letter writing. St. Anselm wrote letters full of warmth and overt expressions of love. St. Bernard wrote volumes of letters, ranging from fierce scoldings to the most dulcet expressions of affection. There was a great flowering of monastic friendships in the 12th century. Of course, we know of one of the most passionate and saddest love stories of all time through the letters that passed between the teacher Abelard and his pupil, the nun Heloise.

These exchanges offer us vignettes into the personal lives of a bygone age. They tell us what monks thought and felt, what was of immediate concern to them, and what they cherished in a relationship. I fear such history of our own time is destined to be lost. Where will any of that be found when emails are so quickly deleted? Even archived emails can be lost in a computer crash. If you save emails on "the cloud," the cloud can crash as well. Will history know as much about modern monks as we know about our medieval brothers?

I am happy for your invitation and this opportunity to re-devote myself to letter writing. We will follow where the Spirit leads us—to fancy or to foundational truth. After all, the earliest writings of the New Testament were letters. St. Paul's missives to the Thessalonians were written well before any of the Gospel narratives. I do not anticipate that ours will prove as transformative or last anywhere near as long, but perhaps we can gain—and offer—some enlightenment for mind and heart.

Yours on the journey,
Br. Paul

Dear Brother Paul,

I am glad we share a mutual zeal for letter writing! We get to know ourselves better through letters. They are one of the last defenses against our false notions of self. The poet Willie Perdomo once observed that it is hard to filter our lives in letters. We can only "attempt to tell the truth and wait."

As I review the narrative of my own life, I find that letters form a kind of underlying soundtrack. The best of them progress from the necessary first movement of monologue to the delightful interplay of dialogue. I have chronicled my travels in letters, declared my love, excused my actions, confided my fears, expressed my hopes, celebrated my successes, lamented my regrets, and rued my mistakes. Letters are the means by which I rekindle friendships that peter out, and by which distant friends keep the flame of friendship alive.

I have carried some letters with me, like heirlooms, through many relocations. One letter I particularly cherish was sent to me by Katherine Graham, the late publisher of the *Washington Post,* after I wrote to thank her for the summer internship at the *Post* that launched my journalism career. Sadly, however, my original letter to Mrs. Graham is lost.

I kept all the letters my mother wrote to me during my junior year abroad in France. After her death, I found my letters to her in a bundle, secured with a rubber band. The letters describe the paltry breakfasts we were fed in the young women's residence where I stayed (one slice of bread with butter *or* jam, but not both), my first experience eating escargot and rabbit, and the international group of friends I was making— from Laos, Cambodia, Cameroon, the island of Réunion, and many parts of France.

Your experience of awaiting letters from family on certain days of the year reminds me of when I lived at the French version of a YWCA. If one of us had mail, we received a slip of paper in the box where we deposited our room keys at the reception desk. It was a good day whenever Madame de la Rivière, the crusty, dark-haired concierge who sat there knitting like a modern-day Madame Lafarge, handed us a letter.

I wrote many letters back home on onion-skin paper, sent in air mail envelopes edged in blue stripes. I wonder if anyone even makes those air-mail envelopes anymore. Lamentably, if my overseas friends correspond at all now, it is by text or social media and our communications tend toward photos and three-or-four-line messages. There is one exception, however—the eighty-nine-year-old mother of the family I lived with in my final month in France. Maman Bracque still writes in long hand on grid paper, her handwriting a little more quivering and difficult to decipher with each letter. I have a special drawer in which I safeguard all of her letters.

I save all the notes my husband leaves me, and my letters to him—like the one I wrote on our first anniversary, marveling at how seamlessly our disparate lives had joined together. Like you, I can't say I reread letters from the past on any regular basis. I agree that they would likely stir up more emotion than I probably want to experience. There are aspects of my nineteen, twenty-one, or even forty-year-old self that are perhaps best left to memory. Still, it is a comfort to know these letters exist. "Resistance against loneliness" is how Willie Perdomo describes them.

Now we begin this new letter-writing pilgrimage. I promise from the outset never to pour sand over the truth. Let the questions lead us to where they want us to go. I trust it will be a journey of surprises.

Yours on the road,
Judith

WORK

Dear Brother Paul,

I had an extraordinary experience today. I was interviewed for a podcast hosted by author Carl McColeman. When he asked me about my perspectives on silence, on the interior life, and on poetry, I realized how much you had influenced my thinking on all of these topics, and so many more.

My thoughts lately have been less about the interior life than about work, however. I remember you telling me about the struggle you went through when deciding whether to ask the abbot to relieve you of your duties in the monastery kitchen. I am struggling with something similar: How do we know when it's the right time to leave a job?

I recently took a leave of absence from my reporting job so I could go on a speaking tour for my latest book. Now I don't know if I want to go back. I used to love the newsroom where I worked, and was often the first person to arrive in the morning and the last person to leave at night. But I went from that to referring to my work-place as "that toxic dump." It all started when the news director I worked with retired unexpectedly. His replacement immediately started moving me away from investigative reporting and long-form features toward basic news reporting—covering city council and school board meetings and political speeches, the kind of assignments usually given to interns. I began to feel as if my journalistic judgment was constantly being questioned, despite the fact that I had won dozens of awards for my reporting, including two national Edward R. Murrow Awards. This tension has finally errupted into a full-blown crisis that threatens my ability to do my work.

The problem is that I don't yet have another job lined up. I would like to write another book. As we both know, however, writing a book is full-time work and most publishers don't pay anything resembling a full-time salary. So . . . how do I make that leap when all that's on the other side is uncertainty?

Yours, skirting a precipice,
Judith

Dear Judith,

I know in part what you are facing in considering a job change. The part that is unfamiliar to me is the insecurity of possibly being without another job. In the monastery, there is always some gap that needs to be filled with able hands.

I have found something agreeable in just about every job given to me here. You could say that I like whatever work I am doing. One reason is because I do not compare my job with other jobs, or with some other job I imagine I want.

Only once have I begged for a job change—when, as you remember in your letter, I wanted out of the kitchen after thirty-five years as a cook. To some extent, I had held on that long out of stubbornness and a sense of self-congratulation for persisting. I liked the job because it was creative and different every day. The results of preparing a dish were immediate, for better or worse. But as I grew older, I noticed that I became less creative in my kitchen work. My life still had plenty of creativity in other areas; I was writing my memoir and working on poems. But when I began to slow down, I became increasingly dissatisfied with cooking.

So how and when did I decide to withdraw? If I were a truly docile soul, I would have followed the small, still voice that spoke to me one day as I was on my way back to the abbey from the Merton hermitage after spending a week there on retreat. But another side of me wanted to show that nothing could break my persistence after decades in the kitchen. The struggle was not all for naught, however. Having to work with other stressed-out individuals was a learning experience. It helped me develop skill in addressing issues without making the situation worse by giving in to negative feelings and reactions. It also helped me to put myself into others' shoes and consider some of the past injuries that may have influenced their behavior.

A kitchen is a hot and noisy place, the work is time-sensitive, and many things can go wrong. It is not a place for quick tempers. Eventually, just walking into the kitchen triggered my anxiety. Singing has always given me a morale boost, but I even stopped singing. The music went out of the job. I became edgy and distracted as I went about my work. There were things I failed to say or do. As a consequence, I had a head-full of comebacks and retorts that I nursed without expressing them. When it got to the point where I could not clear my mind of this tension, I began to seek an exit.

There is an old saying of the Desert Fathers: "If you do not belong in a place, the place will cast you out." Discerning people have a sixth sense about this—especially women, I think—but it comes slowly to me. One morning, I asked for a sign. And that day so many darned things went wrong in the kitchen that I felt I had received one. Finally, I talked my predicament over with the abbot. He made no promises, but worked behind the scenes to shuffle jobs and get me a change.

And there was prayer. I seldom pray to God for personal advantage; I leave things up to divine providence. But here I was praying out loud—just like a man in the Psalms. I must have really wanted to be heard. Prayer kept me (somewhat) from being reactive, from lashing out and making things worse. I asked God to lend a hand.

After waiting patiently, I received a job to which I had never aspired—making the fudge that we sell to help support the monastery. Three years earlier, I would have found the work insufferable—too routine and boring. But at the age of seventy-five, it was perfect. It gave me time to pray and to think, and sometimes even to sit for a spell between cooking batches. We make 450 pounds of fudge a day. People think it must be a hard job, but it is actually easy.

After I left the kitchen, some of my confrères pleaded for me to come back. And as fate would have it, I am back in that job as of two weeks ago, after two years away. So far, so good. The old work habits are kicking in again, and I hope it goes well. Eventually, I'll want to get back to a quieter job. But that will be up to the Lord.

In your situation, Judith, a change of jobs may seem like jumping off a cliff. If the time is ripe, you can have faith that something will be waiting. The important thing is to keep in tune with your inner needs. Fewer demands from work is better as we grow older. It is a way to begin gathering ourselves for the final stages of life.

Peace in the gap,
Br. Paul

Dear Brother Paul,

Ciao! I write to you from Rome. I came here for a planning meeting of Benedictine Oblates, and now my husband and I are staying on for a few more weeks. It has long been a dream of mine to return to Italy for an extended period, ever since I spent a month in Siena as a student trying to learn the language of my grandparents. The leave of absence from my job gives me the opportunity I have been waiting for. This time, I'm not here to soak up grammar, but rather to immerse myself in day-to-day life—shopping in street markets, buying homemade pasta, and negotiating bargains with vendors. My work will be my writing.

Right now, we are in Cassino, about ninety minutes from Rome, where a distant cousin of mine lives. He is a wonderful person who was, for many years, an elected *consigliere* here. He has arranged for us to stay in a little apartment in the center of town. The refrigerator doesn't work and we only have a few dishes, glasses, and pots, but the apartment has a balcony where we can store our food and is just two blocks from St. Anthony of Padua Church where one set of my grandparents were married. I can walk to evening Mass there. The church's bells kept waking me the first few nights, but now I sleep right through them and would miss them if they didn't sound.

Being far from home has given me some perspective on the decision I have to make about whether to quit my reporting job. Shortly before I left on this trip, I attended a discussion on leadership. Something one of the speakers said has remained with me. She asked: "What would you do if you weren't afraid?" Perhaps fear is the only reason why I don't leave my job. Fear of not finding another position with a decent salary and benefits. Fear that my leaving would be perceived as failure—or worse, caving in.

Interesting that you say your worries about your kitchen job interrupted your sleep. Back home, I was having recurring dreams about somehow not being able to complete my assignments. In one, I was directed to clean the newsroom walls and was concerned that my colleagues would see me doing this menial work. An odd element of these dreams is that I am usually unmarried in them, living alone and feeling very isolated. One of the great blessings of being married or living in community, as you do, is that there is always someone there to lean on, at least in theory—in my case, my beautiful husband, Charles; in your case, the abbot who worked to help relieve you of your kitchen job.

Here in Italy, I haven't had any dreams about work. Like you, I often rehearsed things I wanted to say—none of them very gentle or kind—and let them build up in my mind. And like you, I am slowly realizing that I don't want to work in a place dominated by tension, regardless of its cause. And I am also realizing that compassion doesn't always come easily for me. I have to dig deeply into myself to feel empathy for others.

I still don't know exactly what I will do when my official leave of absence ends, but I feel more confident now that I can forge ahead. I have my writing. And I have been getting a great deal of it done here in Italy without the distractions of running a household, being available for friends, and meeting my many volunteer commitments. This sojourn in Italy is proving to be a blessing, a much-needed pause for me to regain my mental, physical, and emotional equilibrium.

Like you, I find it hard to pray for a certain outcome in my life. And yet, for the past year, I have been praying to be led to the right new work. I haven't yet experienced a clear directive, as you apparently did when you walked out of Merton's hermitage after your retreat. My insights have come as gentle nudges, if not quite signals. They come in the form of requests to guide retreats, or to give talks on my latest book, or to work as communications director for the next congress of Benedictine lay associates in Rome, or as a suggestion to begin a new book for my current publisher. These nudges are perhaps akin to the still, small voice Elijah heard in the desert.

I see that, since we last wrote, you have traveled to Alaska for a conference on Thomas Merton's 1968 visit there. I'd love to hear about your trip. And I especially want to know how being back in the kitchen is working out.

Avanti!
Judith

Dear Judith,

By happenstance, since the last time I wrote you, our community has engaged in a workshop on stress in the workplace. Yes, even in a monastery stress can be an issue. One particular item we discussed pertains to your question about knowing when to withdraw from a work situation. The speaker, who was a psychologist, made several points about the cost of workplace toxicity and its trickle-down effects in our personal lives.

One of the key warnings for me was a modification in my behavior. I was complaining a lot to other people, which is not something I like to do and try to avoid on principle. I once had a reputation of never talking negatively about others. But I had begun doing so to friends from outside the monastery, despite the fact that the monastery code of conduct forbids criticizing other monks to "outsiders." We monks are enjoined to deal directly with the brother involved. I did this to some extent, and sometimes others approached me with apologies. Theirs was the greater virtue to make the first move. Mine was mostly the lesser virtue—to keep quiet and endure.

Another telltale sign was experiencing a loss of motivation and productivity at work. On this score, I could claim that, after thirty-five years in the kitchen, I'd had enough. That was my main appeal in asking for a job change. And the abbot understood that, as well as other things. Now, two years later, I have been asked to return to the kitchen. Well, you take what comes.

Fortunately, now that I am back in the kitchen, it feels like a second youth. Our big kitchen requires a lot of pacing about, a lot of lifting and chopping, and a steady choreography to keep up with it all. This is good for the body—better in that regard than fudge-making, which requires precise, repeated arm and leg motions that eventually made my joints ache. On return to the kitchen, I quickly got up to speed, with helpful reminders from the other cooks. And as a bonus, I am enjoying teaching a new cook, a novice who is a natural for the job.

A new monk with whom I have worked in the past is in charge of the kitchen and I like his style. Of the five bosses I have had over the years, he is the best. He doesn't take things too seriously and, while helpful, he leaves you room to do things your own way, which certainly improves motivation. My other bosses (interior cellerars, as *The Rule of St. Benedict* calls them) were usually assigned to other jobs after five or ten years, but somehow I remained. I guess I just wore them all out. Nonetheless, I have no ambition to remain in the kitchen indefinitely. I hope my return is temporary, just as the abbot indicated.

You ask about Alaska. It was not a place I ever dreamed of visiting or had any particular desire to go see. Given my Trappist vow of commitment to an essentially cloistered life, such travel seemed unthinkable. It remained that way until I received a phone call inviting me to give a talk at the first-ever Merton conference in Alaska. The conference drew 400 people, which was a happy surprise. Merton had traveled to Alaska hoping to find a site for a hermitage. My well-informed host knew both of the sites Merton considered, and neither would have been suitable. One was accessible only by air, and the other occupied low land that not even the indigenous tribes would tolerate. Frankly, I cannot imagine that Merton would have suffered to live there.

I was given leave to spend a few days hiking while there. As we drove north toward the immense mountains, I found myself repeating the verse from Psalm 89: "Before the mountains were born or the earth or the world brought forth, You are God without beginning or end." Golden leaves were still lingering on the trees, something that apparently *never* happens there in October. The quaking aspens and yellow cottonwoods added to the magnificence of the mountains, the water, the green spruce, the shrubbery, and the flawless blue sky. We visited sites that Merton had photographed: Matanuska glacier and the quaint old St. Nicolas Orthodox Church where both natives and Russians are buried, each according to their own customs. The indigenous people build little houses on top of the graves, like painted doll houses, each in a different form. One looked like a barn, another like a home. We also saw some Jewish graves with the Star of David on them, or a depiction of the Ark of the Covenant being carried in procession.

Most likely, I will never revisit Alaska, but I tell people that everyone should go there. It leaves an imprint on the soul.

Your less than perfectly stable monk,
Br. Paul

Dear Brother Paul,

It's heartening to hear that monks also encounter some of the same workplace struggles as those of us in the secular world.

As I reflect on my own situation, I find myself wondering if what propels both professional and personal relationships toward brokenness is fear. Fear of fueling anger or, worse yet, facing humiliation. I appreciate your acknowledgment that you haven't always been the person who makes the first overture.

Another question I grapple with is whether I care enough about my job to want to return to it. I have the overwhelming sense that I've done all of the investigative reporting, interesting interviews, and human-interest features that I want to do. I haven't any goals left to fulfill. When I picture in my mind what it might feel like to walk back into the newsroom, I have a hard time imagining myself there. Perhaps God is leading me forward to something new and I am reluctantly hiding in a corner, afraid to press on.

It will take time to write another book and establish a following for my talks and retreats. And I want things to happen *now*. I should know better. I have been in this place before. After I left *The Wall Street Journal* London bureau, I didn't know exactly what I would do. I only knew I needed a break from daily journalism. It took a good two years for things to fall into place. During that time, I went to graduate school for an MFA in creative writing. Within the span of a few years, I wrote two poetry collections and four books on spirituality, and then launched a career in broadcast journalism. I never would have accomplished any of those things if I had kept working at *The Wall Street Journal*.

Friends tell me that I seem fatigued when I talk about journalism, but that I come alive when I talk about the retreats I am leading and the spirituality writing I'm doing. I've been thinking about Merton's writings on the "true self"—not the self we think we should be or that others say we are, but the person we were created to be. A self in a continuous state of discovery. The writer of the Book of Revelation refers to it as our "true name," known to God and waiting for us to discover. I find myself asking: Who am I, really? Who is the self beyond the resumé?

When I was asked to interview you once at a conference on Merton, I couldn't help but notice that your bio

was one of the shortest in the program. The rest of us—
myself included—furnished a long list of our so-called
accomplishments. Some even included the TV shows on
which they'd been interviewed. These are the markers
we use to measure our worth. We think these things are
what make us who we are. You were arguably the most
important person at the conference—the only one who
had actually known Thomas Merton. Yet your bio was
the simplest. A lesson in humility, or at least evidence that
you've moved beyond needing to recite a litany of accomplishments to prove your self-worth. It is enough to be
Paul Quenon, monk.

In his essay "The Root of War Is Fear," Merton says
Christians ought to be able to walk toward the future in
hope. Hope allows us to step into the unknown without
feeling that we are leaping off a ledge, but rather that we
are *learning to walk on air*. That is what I seek. To walk
on air.

Thanks for sharing your reflections on Alaska. It is
the one state in the Union I haven't yet visited. The way
you describe it, I must go. Funny to think that Merton
considered settling where others could reach him only by
helicopter, places where not even the indigenous people
dared to live. He must have wanted his solitude very
badly.

Your ever-perplexed,
Judith

BEING AND DOING

Dear Judith,

I recently asked a young woman, a lawyer who was here
on retreat, how she determined when it was time to leave
a job. She said it is like deciding to leave a relationship.
Although you may still be together, you have an increas-
ing sense that something is no longer working. The
breakup may not exactly occur because you are angry.
The motive comes from a deeper place. It speaks of self-
knowledge—a sense of how you function and how you
don't in a given situation. It implies that you trust in life
enough to believe that another relationship—or another
type of work—is out there to be found.

   I appreciate your readiness to take the long view of
life and see what sparks your enthusiasm now—com-
pleting a new book, lecturing, having time to be quiet
and reflect. This is the moment to ask yourself what you
want to do with the rest of your life. If you do what you
love, you will find the where-with-all. Or as the title of a
book by Marsha Sinetar puts it: *Do What You Love, The
Money Will Follow.*

   What I love is living the monastic life. Part of that is
doing what you are told. Once committed to that basic

acceptance, I tend to like whatever I am doing at the time, whether cleaning the johns, singing in the choir, or writing poetry. No one ever asked me to write poetry. It evolved. It has been, you might say, a love within a love—a love I have nurtured within my monastic vocation. Journalism has been your great love. Now you may be ready for a love within that love, another kind of writing.

I once received a golden nugget of wisdom from an accomplished New Testament professor who had been president of Catholic Theological Union. When I studied there in the mid-1970s, the school was housed in an old eight-story hotel, but the school has now built a spacious new modern building across from the old one. When I congratulated the professor on how much progress he and the school had achieved during his tenure, he replied with something his parents had told him: "Put one foot in front of another and take one step at a time." His parents were wise.

Of course, going step by step implies that you have a goal in view and faith that you can reach it. My long-view goal is to live like a certain monk in a monastery in Georgia who, when he reached the age of 105, was still working and coming to community prayers. I once aspired to lead a similar life, until I started wondering what an awful state the world might be in by the time I got that old! No need to expound on that.

The basic issue, I think, is *change*. I hope I don't get to be the kind of old man who lives in nostalgia for the past. At my age, I have a lot of past to mull over, but my focus is on the present. It is basic to my prayer life and essential to contemplation. My daily meditation practice orients me to focus on the *now* where God is present, whether I feel that presence or not. In any case, eternity is totally present to the now. It is an all-inclusive *now*. As Emily Dickinson says: "Forever is composed of nows."

Stability of place is one of the three vows monks take, along with the vows of obedience to an abbot or prioress, and conversion of life. I am inclined to qualify this and say that monks should also take a vow of commitment to change—a vow of *un-stability*. Almost everything has changed on every level since I entered Gethsemani in 1958. The buildings have been modernized, while the size of the community has shrunk. The people who were here when I entered have either died or left. A few from my early years remain, but the majority of monks here now came later. The liturgy has gone from Latin to English. The music is good, but not the same. The diet is fuller, the rooms more comfortable, and the atmosphere in some ways less noisy. Good changes, mostly. We have also gone from a partly agricultural economy to a mail-order business of fruitcake and fudge. If you live in a monastery and are unwilling to change, you will become dissatisfied, fixated, and isolated from the rest of the community.

Our Trappist monasteries in Ireland provide an interesting example of the complexity of stability. They have so few men joining them today that they have decided that the best way to survive is to combine with other communities, much like parishes are combining in

America. When the Order's leaders proposed this, most everyone agreed it was a good idea. But when it came down to voting to move from one monastery to another, only one person was willing to do it. Perhaps they should have followed a vow of *un-stability*, at least in terms of obedience to circumstances. I can totally understand the feeling of these monks. That is why I resist getting too attached to my own monastery. That kind of attachment can be just as much an obstacle on the way to God as any attachment to the pleasures of the world.

The tone of my life in the monastery is one of being "homeless at home." I have felt that for a long time and, eventually, this feeling took the form of sleeping outside every night. As you know, I get away from the main buildings to a covered porch in an outbuilding that is mostly dry and somewhat protected from the wind. I love the solitude this brings. But it also brings a sense of "having no permanent place on this earth."

I can't claim much bravery in this—I have a really warm sleeping bag that no one is likely to steal. If I were living on the streets, that would be different—as well as dangerous. But overall, this practice is pretty healthy since my body adjusts to the seasons, the air is fresh, and I have fewer colds and flus than in my younger days. I recommend sleeping outside to everybody.

Some feel a need to abandon the monastery altogether to get closer to God as they evolve spiritually. Your decision to make a change in career track could be grounded in the same general principle: Will it get you closer to God?

In this late afternoon of my life, I find myself in a changed state from what came before. I had been living a hidden life—unknown, unheralded, and unsung, as my first abbot often described a monk's life. Now I am published in this country and abroad, and a few people have actually read what I have written, somewhat to my dismay. Was this change in my life my peculiar way of getting closer to God? Only God knows.

What I can say is that I lived with the feeling that I had been given so much in this life that it was time to give in return. I hope I am closer to God through my writing—a hope that springs from the same faith I had while living the hidden life. You know that faith obscurely by experiencing it and living it out in hope. What I am doing with these little poetry books seems right to me. It enhances both my day-to-day life and my inner life; it doesn't distract from my inner life.

If you make a life change now, you will have a simple feeling that it is the right thing to do—if it is, indeed, right. If it is not, you will need to be willing to change course again, or simply to obey the circumstances.

Yours in the struggle,
Br. Paul

Dear Brother Paul,

At 2:20 PM today, I officially resigned from my position. It came down to a simple matter of signing my name on a sheet of paper and filling in the date. Five years of recording dozens of news scripts, conducting hundreds of interviews, and typing thousands of words came to a silent end. When I walked out of Human Resources into the crisp January air, I turned to my husband and said: "Free at last; thank God Almighty, I'm free at last."

No sense of regret. Just relief. The hardest part, perhaps, was working up the courage to make the initial phone call to Human Resources. I rattled on about all the new opportunities I have: working on another book, preparing for dozens of speaking engagements, being invited to teach a class in Rome. I felt I had to reinforce somehow that I have *something important* to do going forward. I suppose this is part of the particularly American illness of judging ourselves not by who we are, but by the work we do.

A part of me wishes I had made the decision sooner, but I was too scared. Now that the decision is behind me, I have a chance to focus on nourishing my mind, body, and spirit. I attend daily Mass now, something I didn't have time for when I was working full-time. I do four hours of fitness classes each week and am taking a class in advanced Italian.

Some days, I break from the writing and spend the afternoon in the kitchen cooking up recipes I discovered on our recent stay in Italy. I can have lunch at home now with my husband. I even enjoy cleaning the house. I've thought about why you titled your memoir *In Praise of the Useless Life*. There are days when I feel totally inefficient, "useless" to use your word. It's somewhat refreshing.

There have been a few "signs" that I am on the right path. I thought I might regret not being able to conduct interviews or do investigative reporting. Then I had an interesting experience. I helped arrange a panel discussion with people in our community who have experienced poverty. Because, for me, journalism has always been a calling, I thought that I'd react by feeling that I had to tell these stories, that I had to make the community aware of how people are suffering. But, although I was deeply moved by the struggles that the people on the program shared, I had a strong sense that *I* didn't have to be the one to tell about them. Others can tell these stories. I can make a different kind of contribution now, through my books and through my retreats.

I see a retired nursing-home aide each day at Mass. When he learned I was a writer, he asked me to write down the titles of my books. Since then, he's bought all of my books and brings them, one by one, to Mass for me to sign. But here's the thing I want to tell you about him. The first time I met him, he pulled a stack of pink cards from his shirt pocket. They were printed with a short poem called "I Said a Prayer for You Today." The poem ends with these lines:

> I asked for happiness for you
> in all things great and small.
> But it was God's loving care
> I prayed for most of all.

I didn't even read the card when he first gave it to me; I just thanked him and stuck it in my purse. The evening I resigned from my job, I noticed its pink edges sticking up from a corner of the purse. I finally pulled it out and read it. I had to smile at the thought of this man's generosity in giving others these prayer cards. I realized that this is his ministry, his way of being "useful."

Another sign. A friend from Mount St. Scholastica Monastery in Atchison, Kansas always carried a pocketful of Kennedy half dollars. Whenever I saw him, he placed one of the coins in my hand. I came to think of these half dollars as good-luck charms for my writing and I kept them on my desk. This past week, my friend died at the age of eighty-two from complications of a stroke he had suffered years before. He never wrote books, or made headlines, or accomplished any hugely useful feat. His main accomplishment was kindness. In this too-often cruel and fractured world, being kind represents quite a big accomplishment.

I have thought about what you said at the end of your last letter—whether the change we seek brings us closer to God. I don't know that the decision to leave my job will indeed do that. I only have an odd sense that it will. Is that faith? Is it hope? I am aware of how blessed I am. I know there are people just as miserable as I was at my job who, because of financial constraints, soldier on. They can't just leap into the unknown. I think of those folks every day.

In faith and hope, yours,
Judith

RESURRECTION
AND POETRY

Dear Judith,

It is often said that the best things in life can't be acquired with a bank account or a credit card. Or to be more correct, I should say the best things in life cost everything. I am thinking of Emily Dickinson's thoughts on the "market price" of life, which she declared to be "precisely an existence."

Yesterday brought me a free gift: a long gentle rain. I perched on my broad, deep windowsill, propped up my feet, leaned on the lintel, and watched the rain drop freely as I read. I could have ignored the rain, but took it as a gift of the moment. After I had read a few pages, the rain stopped and the humid air hung with silence as after a long day's work well done. Have I "paid an existence" for this? Yes. I gave myself to the monastery where such moments are plenteous. There are hard moments as well, requiring self-abandonment for the sake of others. I live for both.

Being outdoors brings its own surprises. Last night, the light rain turned into fine snow and blew under the roof of the porch where I sleep. I felt it on my face, then slept while it accumulated on my sleeping bag. Thanks to that, the bag grew warmer, not colder, for the snow insulated me from the wind.

The real challenge was to rise on time and get out of the bag rather than stay in it. A uniform mother-of-pearl white illuminated the fields, the sky, and the gauzy atmosphere under a full moon hidden by clouds. To see a sight like this is rare. You must be there. It is a good place in which to finger my prayer beads and feel that life *is*.

With gratitude for life and all its surprises,
Br. Paul

Dear Brother Paul,

We live in a world drenched in mystery and wonder, as you have often reminded me. I feel it too, viscerally, yet easily forget. I fill my days with whirls of activity—some of it necessary, much of it not. Sometimes dusk arrives and I've engaged in so many distractions that I can't remember exactly how I spent my time. My precious day disintegrates into a blur, and I find myself flailing around, wasting time, unable to find a proper rhythm. There are days when I don't write a word. Instead, I distract myself with small, ultimately insignificant tasks. This or that email needs a response; this bookshelf needs reorganizing; these clothes need to be washed. A hundred tiny allures that add up at the end of the day to essentially nothing.

In one of her interviews, poet Mary Oliver talks about her vision of death as a re-ordering of our atoms, the way a sapling will sometimes rise where ashes have rested, or new shoots will emerge from a compost of orange rinds and egg shells. It is the idea that all objects contain energy capable of being transformed into other forms of energy. I like that. I've never quite gotten my arms around the Christian belief that, in dying, we are "born to eternal life," as lovely as that sounds. Nor can I say I truly understand what the gospels tell us of Christ's Resurrection. Does it involve a resurrection of the body in its current form, or does it mean a refiguring of atoms we can't in our current life even imagine? A friend of mine who is a Benedictine Sister used to say: "We don't know what happens to us after death, we just *believe*." In your own poem, "Cemetery Walk," you talk about expecting one day to be placed in the ground's "silent keep." Socrates thought our death marked an entry into a vast nothingness or else a profound sleep.

In her poem "Long Life," Oliver asks what it means that the earth is so beautiful, and what we should do about it. What is the gift we should bring to the world? What is the life that we should live? These are the questions I am asking myself as I enter this next chapter of my writing life, jettisoned from the secure way station of my long career in journalism into a new universe, feeling somewhat as if I'm walking in space without a tether.

Warmly (despite our current frigid temps),
Judith

Dear Judith,

I think of death as an entrance into the totality of everything. Therefore, our whole approach to the idea of
heaven and of resurrection just might be on the wrong
footing. We start out asking: What's in it for me? But if
you keep this self-interest up front, you can never get
to the goal. Hope becomes a pretense, a façade, for you
inevitably remain trapped in the little jailhouse of yourself. You just expect that a few conveniences may be
added someday—some landscaping and better ventila-
tion, some upscale amenities.

That is why I rarely think about heaven. Because
it always comes down to thinking of what I would like,
what would suit me, and that as a goal is too small.
To gain the totality, you must give totally of everything.
Every person is made for nothing less than "the everything." Speculating on what that means ahead of time is
not helpful. Really, who knows what it may look like?

As for resurrection, I am still trying to figure that one
out. Resurrection of the body still seems to imply the con-
tinuation of some kind of finite existence. Or maybe not.
Jesus says: "I am the resurrection and the life." Resurrection then is a *person*. As I unite with the person of Christ,
I unite with all persons with whom he is united. Indeed,
as Christ embraces the whole cosmos, then the "totality"
of the cosmos becomes mine in Christ. Certainly a big
payback—way beyond what Emily Dickinson calls "a
single dram of heaven" and way beyond my capacity to
absorb as I now am. That is why I subscribe to the notion

of St. Gregory of Nyssa and some Cistercian Fathers
that we will endlessly enlarge our capacity as we drink
in more. This a very dynamic idea of heaven that goes on
until there is no longer an "until."

I like how St. Paul puts it: Then God will be "all in
all." This eventuality will follow on the great final "giving
over" by Christ of his full authority to the Father. At that
point, God becomes *all in all*. Since that "all" includes
this little bit of flesh I inhabit, then this particle itself will
not only be *within* the all; it will be *comprised of* the all.
The all within all.

There are many ways of understanding the Resurrection—or no way. This is the one that occurs to me
today from a few verses of scripture that lately caught
my attention. To think of my atoms recycling in nature
is small comfort, except as a metaphor of hope. I am
not my particles; they are all renewed every seven years.
I believe that, in death, I will not lose my humanity; it
will be enlarged and more truly what it is. Christ came
to earth as the "new man" to teach us how to be human.
The Resurrection is a further step in that teaching. Something larger and greater. In my present state of being, I
am still an infant in the womb. Our full reality is yet to be
discovered.

There is much of the Resurrection in our love of the
world and of the beauty that nature presents. In loving
nature, in loving the world, we love something larger
than ourselves, and we are made larger by that loving.
So yes, for me it comes down to particular moments and
particular things. This grasshopper, this one nibbling at

my finger who likes the salt on my skin. That black moth
that flew through my window last evening and landed on
my book. Right then and there on February 3rd, when
moths have usually not yet emerged.

Some think that we waste our time walking along the
ocean, gazing at wild geese in the sky. We know better.
Indeed, a good way of getting over the feeling that you are
wasting your time is to go out and waste more of it. Waste
it intentionally. Take a walk in the neighborhood and see
the trees; notice how people keep their yards. Smell the
air. Get free of what seems urgent and necessary; get away
from the feeling that the world will crumble without you.

This may or may not lead to writing something
inspiring. I go through fallow periods and feel no anxiety
about it, like the farm fields that need time in which nothing seems to happen. But below ground, the microbes,
insects, and millions of bacteria that make good soil are
at work. Out of sight. Out of mind, the heart works and
the imagination ferments.

I seem to be in the middle of a pause myself these
weeks. I do not even write haiku, which is good conditioning for longer things. If there is any conditioning
going on now, it is conditioning in waiting things out.

"By your patience you will win your soul" (Luke 21:19),

Br. Paul

Dear Brother Paul,

Your last letter leaves quite a bit for thought. I'm glad
you rarely think about heaven. For centuries, Christian

churches glorified "the afterlife" as if this earthly life were mere excrement. I suppose it was a way of giving hope to the oppressed that their lives will not always be so miserable. I suspect it was mainly a way of mollifying them without actually helping them.

You seem to suggest there is so much more to the Resurrection than is contained in Christian teaching. The Resurrection is perhaps not an event at all, as you say, but a person, Jesus. It means being united in some way with the Christ, but also with all persons, and ultimately with the whole cosmos. Your thoughts reminded me of the awe that astronauts experience in deep space. I like to think of my little particles as being part of the totality of unfathomable space. What separates my atoms—or your atoms, for that matter—from the dark matter of outer space? Or from these computer keys on which I type? Or from the air I am breathing? Or from the trees and clouds I see outside my window?

I once attended a retreat given by a former Vatican astronomer who pointed out that the carbon, hydrogen, helium, and other elements found in the earliest stars form the building blocks of all life, passed down in a continuous chain. Our skin thus contains a remnant of those ancient stars. So does the ground we walk on, and all other living things. This notion cheers me whenever I brood over my "stupid mistakes." It helps me remember that I am not terribly essential to the smooth functioning of the universe, only an infinitesimal part of the whole. My one action won't upset the balance. But in the end, you are quite right. There is not one way of understanding resurrection; in fact, it is more than likely that there is no way at all. Still our experience of being here seems quite a bit more than Ms. Dickinson's "dram" of existence.

I appreciate your counsel that what I consider a waste of time may not be that at all. Perhaps what I need is a kind of mental Sabbath. As you advise in your letter: Waste time, but waste it intentionally. I always thought it interesting that St. Ignatius directed his Jesuits to take a sabbatical every few years to let the mind lie fallow. I think you would have been proud of me a couple of times this week. Twice, I actually napped in the middle of the day. I felt sleepy one afternoon as I was writing at my computer, so I lay down on the couch. What we commonly call here in the Midwest a "stink bug" (though it isn't stinky) began buzzing frantically around the light fixture overhead. Who knew these bugs could survive this late into winter? I don't know how it got into the house. I watched it whirl and whirl for several minutes, then wrote this haiku:

> Frenzied insect guest
> Buzzes around ceiling light
> While I below, nap

My afternoon turned out to be the inverse of what is normal for me. Usually it's the crows, squirrels, and cats of the neighborhood who are the unhurried ones. Today, I was the one lolling around.

I've decided to work on some poems tomorrow. I've been accumulating little scraps of writing that haven't yet coalesced into any kind of whole. If I don't finish a poem tomorrow, will I have wasted that time? I guess you would say not, as long as I wasted my time *intentionally*. As you point out, the seeds, microbes, and mycorrhizae beneath the surface of the hard winter soil may seem to be inactive, but they are silently going about their work, out of sight. Perhaps, as you suggest, something similar happens in the quiet, waiting heart.

I've always loved how St. Benedict, in his *Rule* for monastics, stresses listening. In essence, listening is a kind of waiting—a suspension of activity in favor of being. Perhaps waiting is also a conditioning, like my fitness exercises that are easier at the beginning of the workout and gradually build in intensity until, without realizing it, I become capable of increasingly strenuous exercise. Perhaps patience does win our souls, as Luke says. I will make this my practice in the coming days and see what happens.

Yours in halting patience,

Judith

Dear Judith,

A bit more on the idea of heaven. I don't subscribe to the Marxist notion of heaven as an instrument of class oppression. In some circumstances, it may be so. But belief in an afterlife is found in the most primitive tribal cultures and seems to be intrinsic to the human psyche in its natural state. I once dreamt of my twin sister a year after she died. She showed up in the chapel here at the monastery, and we went to the inner courtyard garden, which seemed, in the dream, more lush and more beautiful than ever. I said: "You were supposed to be dead. Were you away with some man?" She stood there mute, then said: "He is a kind of healer. They say he once died."

Our dreams and ideas of heaven are inevitably too small, given what we now know of the mind-boggling vastness of the universe. Heaven could be no less than that. I just ran across a poem by Walt Whitman that is much to the point for us living in the space age.

> O thou transcendent,
> Nameless, the fibre and the breath,
> Light of the light, shedding forth universes,
>   thou centre of them . . .
> Swiftly I shrivel at the thought of God.
> At Nature and its wonders. Time and Space
>   and Death.
> But that I, turning, call to thee O Soul, thou
>   actual me.
> And lo, thou gently masterest the orbs,
> Thou matest Time, smilest content at Death,
> And fillest, swellest full the vastnesses of Space.
> Greater than stars or suns. Bounding, O Soul,
> Thou journeyest forth.

I like to think that heaven is simply this present world seen from the perspective of eternity and contained in eternity—the mind more vivid and powerful than anything we experience of mind now, or for that matter, of love.

Yours in the exploration,
Br. Paul

LIVING AND DYING

Dear Judith,

Since the last time I wrote you, my eldest brother, Leonard, died. He was eighty-nine, a very kind man. Len had been going into a graceful decline for several years, slipping into a gradual dementia that he evidently accepted and that left him with a sweet disposition. When our father died, Len told me he thought that, when you die, they put you in the ground and that is the end of it. I have not heard whether Len suffered any obvious fear of death toward the end. He was already inclined, by his own account, to dispose of himself when the end came, although it did not turn out the way he had imagined. He mused aloud about going to a Colorado mountaintop, lying down on a snowbank, and watching the flakes come down. "They will never find me until spring," he said. I don't know if Len ever revised his views about the finality of death at any time in the last sixty years. He tended not to articulate such things. When his partner of twenty-five years expressed more religious thoughts on these matters, Len just listened and left things at that.

The advantage of celebrating a death with the gathering of family and friends is that you get an overview of a life lived. The life becomes apparent as a whole. I find myself peering more deeply into the terrain of Leonard's life and asking questions that had not occurred to me previously. As I spent time saying the Psalter for him, I suddenly felt that I also had to include others who had died as well. It dawned on me that these people are more themselves now than they ever were. They have stepped away from the drowsiness of the dying process and walked into a clear consciousness.

The whole of life is a dying process, and we waste much of it being something other than what we really are. It is a wandering into the need for this, or away from fear of that. It is an impersonation of whatever role the moment demands. Rarely do we settle in to *be*.

In the larger scheme of things, Leonard is now Leonard; Father Louis is now Father Louis. Sometimes we knew it; sometimes they knew it. God always knows it.

Yours in the mystery,
Br. Paul

Dear Brother Paul,

There is much in my heart, but this letter is perhaps best left brief. The deepest expressions of comfort I can give you are those that remain wordless. I will, however, share the words a friend of mine spoke to me after my father's death: "I am with you in your sadness."

From what you write, it seems that your brother lived a long and fruitful life. Leonardo DaVinci once wrote: "Just as a well-spent day brings happy sleep, so a life well-used brings a happy death." By that measure, it would appear that Leonard experienced a happy death.

Still, it is difficult to lose a sibling. A friend of mine once observed how the death of a parent forces us to confront our own mortality. We become, not just one or two generations removed from those who pass on, but the next in line. That becomes even more evident when we lose a sibling. I have not yet faced that kind of loss. I'm the youngest among my siblings, but I hardly take it for granted that I will live longer than either my sister or my brother.

Just the other day, I was reading Merton's *Conjectures of a Guilty Bystander*, in which he reflects on a famous poem by the Sufi poet Rumi:

> Everyone's death is of the same quality as
> himself:
> to the enemy of God, an enemy;
> to the friend of God, a friend.
> Your fear of death in fleeing from it
> is really your fear of yourself.
> Pay attention, dear soul!

Perhaps we lack an acceptance of death out of anxiety that we have not lived well in life. Living and loving is something at which your brother seemed to have excelled. The amount we love is perhaps the only true measure of a life well-lived. I'm reminded of the Vietnamese monk

Thich Nhat Hanh's writings based on Buddhism's *Five Remembrances*. I have these words of his taped near my work desk: "My actions are my only true belongings . . . My actions are the ground upon which I stand."

As I age, I find myself less afraid of dying. Perhaps that is because I can, at this point, lean into the fullness of my life, as was hopefully the case for Leonard. There is enough history behind me now to say that, while I surely haven't done everything well, I have done some things well enough. Of course, I'd like as much time as I can get. Time to keep writing. Time to keep loving the people I love. I recognize, however, that I've traveled farther at this stage of my life than I have road ahead of me. That makes each moment that lies ahead even more precious.

In the meantime, while we are in this body, the only rational thing we can do is to be who we are and love who we love. With that, I want to take the opportunity here to tell you that I love you, my friend. I will always have deep gratitude in my heart for this correspondence and for our enduring friendship.

Always forward,
Judith

Dear Judith,

Thank you for your honest reflections.

In a big monastery like Gethsemani, there can be as many as three deaths a year. Relationships here are not terribly intimate. They are only enduring and mostly nonverbal, so it is not too hard to face a loss. These deaths

are a healthy exercise in realism—a spiritual practice
that is not thought of as practice, but as a *de facto* training for death through the experience of sitting next to
your brother's open bier. Our formal rite is to have two
monks, in thirty-minute shifts, recite psalms by the body
day and night until the time of the burial Mass. I still
adhere to an older practice of saying the entire Psalter for
a monk who has died.

In the process of doing that, a change occurs. The
recitation interiorizes the relationship I have with the
brother. I go from praying *for* him to praying *with* him.
It is as if the Psalter's words of joy, conflict, and praise
become his words in me. A closeness and an immediacy
is established that is greater than may have been possible when the monk was alive. I especially felt this after
the death of Father Louis. Instead of his being set at a
remove, he began to feel more immediate and closer to
me. A new kind of contact became possible—something
greater than before. Not verbal contact, but rather a kind
of communion. Silence was the place where this could
happen.

Again, the words of Emily Dickinson come to mind.
She tells us that time does not assuage, but that suffering
"strengthens as sinews do, with age." Perhaps there is
some implication in the word "sinews" that we ourselves
are strengthened by suffering. We become more than we
would otherwise have been.

I seldom pray that someone will be spared death.
We all have to die sometime. I only pray that we die
well. Merton died young, at fifty-three, but he died

well I think. His death was shocking and abrupt, but it delivered a remarkable final punctuation to an astonishing life. Would he be quite as memorable without that ending—pinned under a malfunctioning electric floor fan in Bangkok?

Yours in the living,
Br. Paul

Dear Judith,

I return today to the computer to tell you that Brother Patrick Hart died last night. As a young monk, Patrick was Thomas Merton's personal assistant. Over the years, he edited and oversaw the publication of Merton's voluminous writings. Flu and pneumonia defeated him in the end. He stopped eating three days ago.

Patrick was ninety-three, a good age at which to die. It was the end of a very fruitful life that was given over to his many contributions to Merton studies. Patrick began handling mail and manuscripts for Merton in the early Sixties and continued editing and proofing his writing through the decades that followed. His did his last editing work in 2013 for Merton's *In the Valley of Wormwood,* a collection of the lives of Cistercian saints. Although this was the first book Merton wrote at the monastery, it was, ironically, the last one to be published.

There was hardly a question about Thomas Merton that Patrick could not answer. He continued to read new books and studies that came out on Merton until last October when his mind began to fail. He had been secretary to several of our abbots, from Dom James Fox in Merton's time through the early years of Father Elias Dietz, our present abbot. That alone would have represented a remarkable life of service to the monastery.

The day he died was gray and gloomy. A grey day in February is a good day to die. More of our monks have died in February than in any other month. The best I can say is that Brother Patrick lived well. Many can be grateful to him for his kindness and help.

Remembering with gratitude this excellent monk,
Br. Paul

Dear Brother Paul,

This is my first chance to write since returning home from Brother Patrick's funeral. Funny how our recent letters had been circling around mortality and eternity. Then the death of a beloved monk brought us together in person.

I met Brother Patrick only once. He was gracious and gentle-mannered in just the way his fellow monks described him at his funeral. Although I didn't know him well, I felt I owed it to him to be there for the service. People like myself would not have the benefit of so much of Merton's wisdom if Patrick Hart had not collected, deciphered, and assembled so many of his manuscripts.

This was my first experience of a Trappist burial. I haven't stopped thinking about it for days. You once told me that monks are laid directly in the ground without a coffin. One can imagine this, but it is quite something else to witness it. Seeing the body lowered in that way drove home for me how much the flesh represents the shell of a person. Whatever spark had animated Brother Patrick in life was clearly gone.

The hood of Brother Patrick's cowl largely obscured his face. Another sign, I suppose, that the true being is no longer contained in its shell. Several people were standing in front of me, so I didn't have a clear view of everything occurring at the gravesite. All I could see when the body was lowered were Brother Patrick's black rubber-soled shoes. The sight of those shoes filled me with tenderness for the man. I thought of the decades those feet had trod the stone floor of the abbey church or sank into the soft soil of the surrounding hills.

Another image that stays with me is that of the monk who climbed down a ladder into the grave before Brother Patrick's body was lowered on a cloth. You once told me that a community member always goes down there to "accept" the body. The monk then lumbered back up the ladder and out of the grave, like Lazarus resurrected from the dead.

I wonder if you have ever had that task, and what it is like to be confined, even briefly, in that six-foot hole with the lifeless body of a brother monk. What does it feel like to ascend again into the land of the living? I can't help but think that this is a powerful reminder of the brevity and preciousness of life.

For days afterward, I couldn't rid my mind of the image of various insects and animals feasting on Brother Patrick's unprotected body. Ants, beetles, worms, tree roaches, moles, woodchucks, chipmunks, raccoons. I remember letting the undertaker who handled my mother's funeral talk us into purchasing a vault to lock over her already air-tight coffin. Ostensibly, the vault prevents the coffin from floating away in case of a flood. But all I could think of was: "No insect or animal is going to take a bite out of my mother!" So stupid, since our very existence depends on the bites we take out of other living things. I suppose there is serendipity to our own flesh becoming part of the food chain in the cycle of life.

I recently read an essay by Mary Oliver called "Sister Turtle," from her collection called *Upstream*. She describes encountering a red-tailed hawk munching on a pheasant breast and a raccoon devouring "with rapacious and happy satisfaction" nesting turtles by a pond. One day, she reaches into the sand and extracts some buried turtle eggs. She takes the eggs home and scrambles them, commenting that they were "not too wonderful, not too bad." She concludes: "Not at this moment, but soon enough, we are lambs and we are leaves, and we are stars and the shining, mysterious pond water itself." Do you suppose this is yet another meaning of resurrection?

There is another beautiful passage in *Upstream* where Oliver describes lying down in a field and looking up from the level of the grasses, in tune with the plants of the earth and the animals. "I was some slow old fox," she says, "wandering, breathing, hitching along, lying down finally at the edge of the bog, under the swirling rickrack of the trees." This passage reminds me of how you often call nature your "guru" and observe that we humans are merely a part of the community of beings.

Today was the first relatively warm day in what has
been a cold and exhausting winter. I inhaled the tinge of
spring in the air. You know how you can sometimes smell
the change of season? A scent of newness was there, even
though the dry leaves, desiccated grass, and browned
flower heads still seemed dormant. When I came back
inside, I wrote this haiku:

> After snow, cold wind
> Sun returns like one whose name
> I can't remember.

A friend of mine once remarked that it is natural to yearn
for romance in spring. All of nature is giving birth and
the female body also wants to grow something. I laugh
at that now, but maybe she was right in a way. In the
Midwest, spring is a brief and precious time. As the new
crocuses and tulips break through the soil, I too start to
feel younger.

You quoting Walt Whitman in your previous letter
made me think of my favorite lines from *Leaves of Grass*.
They are my call to prayer for the start of this spring:

> Reckless O soul, exploring, I with thee, and
> > thou with me,
> Sail forth—steer for the deep waters only,
> For we are bound where mariner has not yet
> > dared to go,
> And we will risk the ship, ourselves and all.
> O my brave soul!
> O farther farther sail!

O daring joy, but safe! Are they not all the seas
    of God?
O farther, farther, farther sail!

Yes, I suppose we are all bound where the mariner has yet
to go.

Yours in the sailing,
Judith

TIME

Dear Judith,

Another huge loss and the year not yet half over. You no
doubt have heard news of the death of the poet and sage,
W. S. Merwin.

I once wrote Merwin asking him to be a judge of
the annual Thomas Merton Poetry Prize. He wrote back
saying that he would willingly have accepted, but that he
was having trouble with his eyesight. He recalled living
on Perry Street in New York, where he could look down
on the apartment Merton occupied in his student days at
Columbia University.

He also recounted his visit to Merton's hermitage
long after Merton had died. It left him with the impression that Merton still lingered in that place. Many people
sense that, as I do when I am able to spend a week alone
there. Conversations with visitors often turn deeply personal at the hermitage, and I cannot help but credit that
to the spirit of the man who lived there fifty years ago.
This far surpasses standing by his grave in the abbey cemetery. There, the dead just seem dead. Sometimes when I
see visitors standing at Merton's gravesite, I think: "Why

seek the living among the dead?" Words the angel said to
the women at the tomb of Jesus, as you know.

I was never given the task to climb down into the
grave to receive a monk's body. That is the job of the
infirmarian who cares for the sick. I am always topside,
singing. It is a challenge to sing in the cemetery under
the open sky, with no walls or ceiling for reverberation.
My voice seems so small under all that vastness. But
somehow, I feel that I do not have to be anything but
very small, and it is good to be part of a vastness that
goes beyond my space and time. Again we come back to
Emily Dickinson, who describes the "finished feeling" of
gravesites and the "wilderness of size" felt there.

Time rolls on in the monastery after a funeral. Life
is wounded by an absence, but also rounded, more complete. One more life story has gone full circle. It is funny
how monks will remember some peculiarity of a person
they lived with, like brothers in a family. For instance,
the way Patrick would continually clear his throat while
reading in the Scriptorium. It would annoy one of my
fellow monks to no end. I try rather to remember what
was good about the deceased. How Patrick, for example,
had such vigorous interest in people. He often mentioned
someone he thought would be of special interest to them,
like a figure from the literary world whom he knew. Some
found that to be showing off, but I loved it.

In recent years at the monastery, we have begun
having discussions in Sunday Chapter (our community
meetings) after a funeral. There, we sometimes hear personal accounts of a monk's finer moments or learn things

we had not known about him before. I hadn't known that Patrick had trained as a vet and had once tended the cows at the abbey. It doesn't fit our image of him as the man behind the typewriter. Many also did not know that he played classical piano but dropped it, he told me, because he had trouble remembering. We never saw him play here.

From a temporal point of view, all this has disappeared into the past. But from the eternal perspective, I like to think that none of this is lost. Eternity is present to all time—past, present, and future. It is all there; nothing is lost. Each person is in the heart of God, as the person they were in their own space and time. Or rather, as the person they *are,* in their own proper being, in God's timeless consciousness, which excludes nothing of the particular and the temporal. "He is not God of the dead but of the living, for all live to him." (Luke 20:38)

Usually, I am aware of only one particular sliver of time. One "now" after another "now." I take this for what it is, but I err if I take it for *all* that is. Within the real, there is what leads to the more real, and of that there is no measure. I am most aware of this in meditation, where being present to the moment is most important. It is a consecration of the moment that is, of moments present all the time. Individual moments are swept away from our awareness in the course of a day. By pausing and returning to time, we can open onto a deeper dimension of time. This depth does not prove that time is an illusion. Rather it takes time for all it's worth, as in "the fullness of time." For that there is no measure.

Last month, I wrote a poem about this, which I named "Seashell of Time":

This moment, cast up on your shoreline,
is from the sea of time.
Hold it to your ear and listen.
The whole ocean is inside sounding.
Within each moment
tides of hours are surging.
Within each hour fathoms of years.
Do not discard this present moment.
It curls inward to resounding canyons.
Hold the precious conch shell a while and
    listen.
It's awash with centuries
beneath centuries awash.

I resist saying time is an illusion. Our measure of time is an illusion when we take that as what time is. When you take a break and forget the time for a while, you are actually recovering time for the fullness that it is, no longer parcellated by our measure.

In modern monasteries, time is measured by clocks; but in the Benedictine *Rule,* time is more organic. It is measured by the sun. The winter schedule is different from the summer schedule. Someday we should institute a reform in which we banish all clocks from the monastery. All that will remain is a bell in the tower that announces when to gather for services. The bell ringer will have a sundial and a native instinct for cloudy days. Or perhaps we should go on authority, and let the abbot ring the bell. That, in fact, is what is specified in *The Rule*. In that circumstance, it is not a motor that determines my time; it is a person. How would you like that?

Yours beyond the bounds of time,
Br. Paul

P. S. It might also depend on how much you like the abbot.

Dear Brother Paul,

Once again our minds seem in sync. I too have been thinking about the nature of time. Particularly intriguing is your idea that time is not an illusion; rather it is our *measurement* of time that is illusory. I sensed a bit of that this afternoon as I grew fatigued working at my computer. Instead of forging ahead, battling the tiredness as I usually do, I lay down on a couch and closed my eyes, expecting to take a short nap. I woke up three hours later. Strangely, however, I had the sense when I awakened that time had slowed, and that I hadn't missed anything at all by not pressing on with work.

The long-ago monastic schedule did not need clocks, as you point out, only the sunrise and sunset, the slant of light and shadow, and the ringing of bells. I stopped wearing a watch years ago on the theory that there are enough clocks around—in the car, on buildings, in public plazas. The face of every cell phone now streams the hour, making watches largely obsolete, so we stay tethered to our phones as if they were some postmodern version of a phylactery.

I am learning to discern the hour by becoming attuned to the progression of light and shadow. I can often tell when it is around 6:15 in the morning, the time I like to wake up, by the rim of light seeping through the bedroom shades. I can guess when it's about 7:15 in the evening by the position of the setting sun (harder to do on cloudy days). In a radio interview, author Pico Iyer described experiencing something similar while living in Japan. "The biggest luxury I enjoy when I'm in Japan is, as soon as I arrive, I take off my watch and I feel I never need to put it on again," he said. "I can soon begin to tell the time by how the light is slanting off our walls at sunrise and when the darkness falls."

Still, I can get caught up in conventional measures of time. Like some obsessed actuary, I have begun to look ahead trying to forecast how many years I may have yet to live. There are surely fewer ahead than behind me. I find myself grieving over what I didn't accomplish in the last several decades and lamenting that I may not have "time enough" to do what I'd like to do in the time that remains.

This, of course, leads to an inevitable question: What have I accomplished? And does what I have accomplished amount to much? In your memoir (for which Pico Iyer wrote the foreword), you praise the "useless life." The question that haunts me is: What if my life turns out to be useless?

As a journalist, I used to feel a sense of accomplishment whenever I reported a story that made a difference in people's lives. Inevitably, however—and fairly quickly—the memory of those articles crumbled like the dried flowers we try to preserve between the pages of a book. Does anyone remember the interview I conducted with Broadway composer Jerry Herman? Or the investigative series I reported on police and race? Or the article I wrote on Native American Catholics reclaiming their ancient traditions? Even I have forgotten many of these articles and interviews. Useless?

You offer an interesting anecdote about this in *In Praise of the Useless Life* when speaking about your early days in the monastery. An older monk told you that the contemplative life "is not a matter of sitting under a shade tree." The monk who said that, you note, eventually left Gethsemani. You are still there, sitting under shade trees.

Perhaps I am spending too much time contemplating *myself*. You say Merton warned you about spending too much time looking inward. His general remedy, you tell us, was to "live the life here at the monastery, stop looking at myself, and forget myself." He apparently returned to this advice later in your novitiate when he said: "[I]f you just go through the day and do your work . . . growth will happen."

Thank you so much for sharing with me your poem, "Seashell of Time." I'm sending along "Vesper Time," a recent poem of mine that also attempts to cherish the present moment. I wrote it after observing day after day the same elderly couple in Italy. I just learned it has been

selected for honorable mention in this year's Merton
Poetry of the Sacred Contest. That means a great deal
to me.

> This is how I learned to love:
> watching an aging couple
> climb the twenty-five stairs
> from Spoleto's old quarter
> to the new, even on a day
> so hot a dropped egg
> fried on the stone steps.
> Every afternoon at five,
> they arrived at the *gelateria,*
> he nearly blind, she guiding
> him by the arm, ordering
> one scoop between them,
> some days *nocciola,* others
> *pistacchio* or *amarena.*
> Always at the same table,
> she dipped a plastic
> spoon in the paper cup
> and he opened his lips,
> received her offering
> like a communion wafer.
> Rarely talking, only looking
> into each other's eyes.
> Then they headed home
> the way they came
> to a house I imagined:
> painted *espresso* cups

on a cedar table,
lace doilies on sofa arms,
framed image of Santa Rita
di Cascia staring from a wall.
Another afternoon adrift
in their calendar of graces.

        Yours in the grace of the present moment,
                                 Judith

PURPOSE AND CALL

Dear Brother Paul,

My graduate school adviser, novelist Rosellen Brown, was in town recently to read from her latest novel, *Lake on Fire*. We had lunch at my home and I told her what you had responded when I asked you about the purpose of the Trappist life in the modern world. "The purpose of the Trappist life in the modern world," you said, "is to show you don't need a purpose. The purpose of life is life and you just have to be." Your words hit me like a shock because they ran so counter to my drive to make a difference. I always took to heart the Greek's definition of happiness—the use of all our talents in the pursuit of excellence. Often in my workaholic phases, I would get the "pursuit" part, but didn't experience the happiness.

Rosellen countered that the purpose of life is to discover your purpose. The protagonist of her latest book is a Jewish immigrant from Russia who leaves her family's farm in Iowa to seek a more consequential life in Chicago. She leaves her former life behind out of a sense that she was made for more. You might say Rosellen's character is pursuing a purpose-driven life.

One of the issues I've struggled with since leaving journalism is figuring out what my purpose is now. I don't think I can be satisfied if the purpose of my life is simply to *be*. I like to take action, to be the heroine of whatever story I am in. You probably would agree that, in the final analysis, your Trappist life has also involved a purpose. I suspect you wouldn't have persevered in the monastery for more than sixty years if it didn't. At any rate, your comment made for a lively conversation with Rosellen.

Yours between purposes,
Judith

Dear Judith,

I draw a distinction between having a purpose and following a vocation. A vocation is beyond what you might call a purpose in life. I did not find a purpose; my purpose found me. I basically live with a sense of a call—and beyond that, a sense of someone calling. The purpose I serve is not so much a purpose as a radical freedom that is rooted in God. It is, I hope, obedience to a freedom that is both mine and one greater than mine.

Life's purposes can be multiple and can change as time goes on. They vary as the will of God makes them for one present moment or another. Life is the art of keeping a harmony in these purposes, maintaining a balance, a serenity that comprises a living symphony of prayer.

One reason why I did not continue studying for a PhD in theology at Chicago's Catholic Theological Union was that, in the city, I lacked the balance I maintained at the monastery. Not that I didn't try to have it there. Here, however, I have a more total life. Studying or writing at school felt like a diminishment. Although I write a great deal here at the monastery, writing, fortunately, has not become my primary purpose. I have no ambition to dedicate myself mainly to writing. That would flop if I tried. For me, writing is primarily a way to enhance the contemplative life I already have.

I share that contemplative life with others within the walls of the community. The writing I share beyond the walls is something of a labor of love. I hear it as a call, something for this stage of my life that comes from the same One who called me to the monastery in the first place. I hope I am hearing this call rightly. If not, it will fizzle out of its own spiritual inertia. Although the other monks like to see my books published because they sense they enhance the community, I doubt many read much of my work.

I can understand the view of your former writing instructor, who must be endowed with a major talent and has dedicated her life to serving art. I would hope, beyond this, that she senses something transcendent. Beyond the pursuit of excellence, whether in work or sport, there is the call to perfection and beauty which is a call *from* perfection and beauty. Perhaps some never recognize this. Perhaps they never name it, but know it in their bones. What you have is something *given*. Even the gift to cultivate what you have is ultimately given.

Much of high culture today is building an altar to "an unknown god." I like what St. Paul says when he enjoins us to dwell on "whatever is true, whatever is honorable, whatever is right, whatever is pure, whatever is lovely, whatever is of good repute . . . and anything worthy of praise." (Philippians 4:8) As a monk, I take this as a well-rounded program for the contemplative (and writing) life.

In love of every excellence,
Br. Paul

THE HUNGRY SHEEP

Dear Brother Paul,

I'm just back from another meeting of Benedictine lay associates at Sant'Anselmo Monastery in Rome, which is both a seminary and the seat of the Abbot Primate of the Benedictines. Instead of returning filled with enthusiasm for my faith, however, I feel conflicted and sad. It all gelled for me one morning at Mass when it suddenly struck me that there were thirty-one men on the altar. Men doing the readings, men singing the responsorial psalm, men giving the homily, men consecrating the Eucharist, men serving Communion. Not one woman.

Why this would bother me *now,* when all my life I've only ever known a male Catholic clergy, I don't know. It might have been the sheer number of men. Women, like myself, were at the Mass in our assigned role as spectators. If we are to believe we are formed in the image of God, then, as it says in Genesis: "God made them male and female." And yet our Church doesn't recognize a call to priesthood in the female image of God.

I don't recall having this kind of reaction the many times I've attended Mass at your abbey, though there are only male presiders there as well. Perhaps it is because there are fewer priests at Gethsemani than at Sant'Anselmo, so the number of men on the altar did not seem quite so overwhelming. Monks who are brothers, like you, sit separately at Mass from the priests. We, the lay people, sit behind the brothers, separated by a wide aisle. A pecking order reigns to some degree at Gethsemani. Another difference is that the abbey church is a part of the monks' permanent home. I suppose they should be able to sit however and wherever they want in their home. At Sant'Anselmo, the majority of monks are on temporary assignment.

The Church's tone deafness can be excruciatingly loud and painful at times. A while back, during a wave of new revelations about clergy abusing children, the pastor of the parish I attend decided to hand out copies of a book called *101 Inspiring Stories of the Priesthood*. A parishioner had donated $4,000 for the purchase of the books. I'm sure that person had good intentions. Still, I can't help but think that $4,000 easily could have paid for a good number of meals for hungry people. It could have covered the legal fees for an undocumented immigrant trying to gain asylum in the U. S. It could have helped pay someone's medical bills, or several months' rent for a struggling family.

The pastor apparently thought it was so important to get this book into the hands of parishioners that he had altar boys pass them out as people returned to their seats from taking the Eucharist, the most sacred part of the Mass. His twenty-minute homily was disjointed to

the point of being incoherent at times. It lurched from
the gospel story of the Epiphany, to a passage from *101
Inspiring Stories of the Priesthood,* to a letter Pope Francis had written to American bishops on the abuse crisis.
I kept thinking of a line John Milton wrote about the
Church of the 17th century: "The hungry sheep look up
and are not fed."

What will save the Church is not heartwarming
stories about 101 good priests. We need reform—real
reform—something akin to the Second Vatican Council
and the Counter-Reformation combined. Everything
should be up for discussion. Priestly celibacy. Women in
the diaconate. Lay input in the choosing of pastors and
the naming of bishops. Lay oversight of Church finances.
And—dare I say it?—women in the priesthood.

We need to carefully, prayerfully read scripture and
ask the right questions. What is it that Christ actually
established? Yes, he appointed Peter to shepherd the
early Church and lead the disciples. But he did not pre-
scribe a male priesthood in perpetuity. He did not decree
that priests should never marry. As someone once joked,
if the twelve apostles are the model for the Catholic
priesthood, then all of today's priests should be married
Jewish men.

It is too facile to attribute the exodus of people in their
twenties and thirties from the pews to self-centeredness or
secularization. People attend church expecting to be fed. If
they walk away still hungering, disheartened by the drivel
coming from a clergy removed from ordinary concerns,
how can we expect them to remain?

I think of the evening you and I went out to dinner
after we both spoke at a Merton conference in Chicago.
Father Richard Rohr, the Franciscan writer, was with us.
You had on sandals, a pair of pants with frayed cuffs,
and the sole civilian shirt you own—a gold one that is
too big for you that you jokingly call your "party shirt."
Father Richard wore faded gray chinos, a flannel shirt,
work boots, and a worn woolen skull cap that covered
the bandages on his head from some recent skin surgery.
No disrespect, but you both would have blended in quite
well with Chicago's many street dwellers. Then, into the
restaurant pranced four young priests in long black cas-
socks looking like Father Guido Sarducci on *Saturday
Night Live*. The French have a saying for folks like that.
They call them: "Moi tu as vu," which translates as "Have
you seen me?' These young clerics might as well have been
shouting: "Hey, look at me! Make way for the priest!"

I doubt these young clerics would have guessed that
the elderly gentleman in the bad-fitting clothes sitting at
the next table was a Trappist monk who'd spent sixty-
plus years in prayer and contemplation. Or that the
gentleman dressed like a longshoreman was a Franciscan priest whose writings have drawn thousands of lay
people to contemplative practices. No inspiring stories
from a book on the priesthood could have done more
than you and Father Richard have done for the Church.
Pope Francis has said that he wants his priests to be shep-
herds who smell of their sheep. No animal scent on these
young priests, just cologne. No sheep scat on their shiny
black Oxfords.

I often say I remain a Catholic because no one is
going to chase me from the Church of my ancestors. I
stay, most of all, because I believe in the real presence of
Christ in the Eucharist. When I attend other churches, the
music may be wonderful, the people may be friendly, and
the sermons may be stimulating, but if there is no Eucharist, there is a void that none of these other things can fill.

Your thoughts? Or perhaps it is best for monks to
float above controversy, or else keep their heads down
and pray.

Beginning to despair of it all, and not wanting to,
Judith

Dear Judith,

In a sense, I have already despaired. Or perhaps you
could say I have hoped against hope. Church history is
full of blunders. Somehow, we survive. God continues to
work around the edges of the shape in which things have
been cast by human hands. Salvation often happens in
spite of us; the real work of the kingdom takes place in
obscurity and in unexpected places.

I am suspicious of people who come out with a
manifesto and make a flourish of denouncing this or
that. I agree with Dorothy Day, who said she never
believed much in popes and bishops who can be venal
and short-sighted. Change often springs from saints and
mystics, but also from the humble and the poor. Such,
for instance, is the renewal of preaching that took place
through two humble men, St. Dominic and St. Francis.

The renewal of preaching led to renewal in the Church, and this is what you long for. It cannot solve all the problems, but it can change attitudes.

As for women's ordination, I once hoped there would be Catholic women priests by now. It hasn't happened. In the 1970s, when I got to know some of the Loretto sisters from the local motherhouse near the abbey and the Sisters of Charity from Bardstown, I found them intelligent, spiritual, and more qualified than some of the priests in our community appeared to be. When I was in school in Chicago, one of the first events I attended was a dinner with a Passionist priest who expressed firm support for women's ordination. Ritual practices can and do change, he claimed, and suggested that women's ordination might best be done regionally, beginning with the U. S. and Europe. That was in 1975.

I somehow assumed that all this would have happened by 2013. That was just a date I pulled out of my head because it seemed far enough in the future. Well, that date has come and gone, and things have gotten more entrenched than before. One of my sisters-in-law—a strong mother of six who is active in her town's politics—left the Church over this issue. At this point, women's ordination is overshadowed by the question of what will become of the priesthood itself. It is necessarily going to change because of the shortage of candidates and the consequent shift of responsibility to lay people and catechists. In the past, the Church in some remote regions of China went without priests for decades, and the people somehow continued their practice of prayer and faith.

In time, the role of priests may change and women may find priesthood undesirable, or unnecessary to what they would like to see occur in the Church. What looks like an urgent problem in our times may eventually become moot. It would be ironic if women obtained the opportunity to take on a role that only men now play just when that role is crumbling to the ground. That is one way of saying that, although I continue to hope, I no longer have a clear image of what I am hoping for.

There is a strong urge among today's younger clergy to restore the image and authority of priesthood. Dressing for the role is part of that. The young priests we saw in the restaurant in their traditional garb might be considered a support team for a group of men who find themselves under a cloud of suspicion. It is over-compensation, perhaps. Like your experience of the books being passed out at Communion that extoled the merits of priesthood, this may just show how desperate things are.

In the truest, deepest sense, priesthood has to be vocation—something more profound than a career, a lifestyle choice, or celebrity status. Some men want to be priests for the prestige. Young people grow up seeing celebrities on television; the priesthood is, in a way, a religious form of the same thing. The clergy crisis has shown us what can become of men who place themselves above others. Women can get hooked on the same bait. We need to be sure that our future priests answer to a much humbler and more interior calling—as it was meant to be in the first place.

Some women believe they have a priestly vocation and want it to be honored and recognized. I sympathize with them. I am confident that many of the priests you saw crowded onto the altar at Sant'Anselmo are of the same mind as I am and would like to see change. But, as you observed, concessions must be made for the monastic liturgy in a community of men. Gethsemani is not that different from Sant'Anslemo. During my first twenty-five years here, lay people—both men and women—had to sit in the balcony of the chapel. At least now we bring them onto the main floor and they can sing with us. The liturgy is by and for the people as well. It took some re-thinking for us to see that. Monastic life, after all, was a lay vocation to begin with. St. Benedict, the major figure of Western monasticism, was not a priest! Priesthood was something extra—something that reflected an interior call as well as a call from the community.

Fifty years ago, Thomas Merton compared our situation in the Church to that of the disciples on the road to Emmaus. We are full of doubts and questions and do not realize that all the while Jesus is walking with us. Merton wrote:

> The core of this kind of doubt is a big question mark, who is right? Today everybody is fighting over who is right. Every side claims to have the answer. This is one of the religious facts of our time. People go into agony. It doesn't matter who's right. God is right, hang on to the Lord at the deeper level, and let all the others yell. The

*fidelity of God is there, and I have to be faithful
to Him and to my fellow man, too.*

These words are even more broadly relevant today,
given the political atmosphere. We are required to have a
deeper grounding in faith and, in a sense, of the transcendent—that God is right. Who am I to make an exclusive
claim to what is right? God is right.

Yours in peace,
Br. Paul

PRAYER

Dear Judith,

From time to time, I have the unique opportunity here at the abbey to greet and visit with Buddhist monks. One unforgettable moment happened years ago when Anne Walters, of the Drepung-Gomang Center in Louisville, brought young monks from India to the abbey, along with her own children.

We went to Merton's hermitage and, while I sat on the porch talking with the monks' spiritual teacher, a game of soccer started up in the yard between Anne's kids and the monks, who were really good at soccer. The color of the saffron robes against the lush green of the yard and the speed and hilarity of the game still lives in my imagination. For me, it was an image of the kingdom of God realized in the present moment—multiple religions coming together in play, joy, and abandonment.

This past week brought another special visit. I escorted the Buddhist teacher Shechen Rabjam Rinpoche to Merton's hermitage. He was accompanied by a few other Tibetan monks and a small group of supporters. Rabjam was in Louisville to officiate at the dedication of a new *stupa*—a peaked, circular structure around which devotees walk and pray—built in honor of Merton and His Holiness the Dalai Lama on the grounds of the Catholic Spalding University. It will eventually include a labyrinth as a companion piece and a Christian symbol. The structure has a cedar post in the center that is rooted in the ground and rises to the peak of the dome. The post of the new stupa is special because it was taken from a red cedar that grew on the grounds of our abbey.

The cutting of this tree was done with great ceremony. Last year, Geshe Kalsang Rapygal came from Louisville and carefully selected the tree. It had to be perfectly straight and thirty to forty feet tall. We drove out to a cedar grove alongside the dirt road leading to Merton's hermitage. Geshe walked into the grove and quickly found the perfect tree. Since this was a gift from the monastery to the Buddhists, I thought it best to ask one of our priests to do the cutting. To make this a truly Christian-Buddhist ceremony, I sang our hymn from the Good Friday liturgy: "O faithful cross, O tree all beauteous." This hymn was later inscribed on the pole, along with texts by Thomas Merton and the Dalai Lama, and various *sutras*. Relics are embedded in the pole, including a relic of the grandfather of Rabjam. Rabjam was born in India and became a monk at the age of five. He was raised by his grandfather, Kyabije Dilgo Khyentse, an outstanding teacher who imbued his grandson with monastic teaching from early youth.

Rabjam is a big man with a face like a moon rising over the mountain. His visit to the abbey took place two days before the dedication of the stupa. On one of those days, we drove to Merton's hermitage for lunch. He chose a shady place on the lawn behind the fifteen-foot cedar cross that stands in the yard as the spot for our small circle to eat. There, we could hear the bells ringing for mid-day prayers. The ringing of the Angelus bell piqued Rabjam's curiosity. As I explained to him how we pray the Angelus, I was reminded of a thought that had occurred to me at Mass that morning—that every Christian is a reincarnation of Christ because we eat his body and drink his blood. He dwells in us. Rabjam understood immediately. Before I finished the words, he put his fingertips to his mouth and recalled that he had once taken Communion when he was at an Orthodox monastery in Romania.

Later, we talked about "the three"—past, present, and future—and "the fourth," which is not those three but includes them. I understood this as being similar to St. Augustine's *toto simul*, everything in one moment—past, present, and future. We also spoke of the remarkable life of Rabjam's grandfather, who spent a total of twenty years living in a cave, interspersed with periods spent in the monastery. Rabjam said he understood very well Merton's desire to gain a distance from the busyness, affairs, and administration of a monastery.

After our lunch at the hermitage, and filled with excitement over my visit with Rabjam, I tried to phone my friend Richard Weingarten to learn if he knew Rinpoche Rabjam. Richard is thoroughly familiar with the Tibetan masters, has been a personal advisor to the Dalai

Lama, and has designed a program for financial support of the Tibetan monasteries in India. I didn't get through on the phone. The next day, his wife emailed me from India to tell me that Richard had died of a heart attack. It happened in Dharamshala, the village of the Dalai Lama, the perfect place for Richard's death. He had gone there every year since 1986 and usually saw the Dali Lama. In fact, the Dalai Lama was present when he died and said a blessing over him.

Suddenly, everything in me slowed to a standstill. It seemed impossible that Richard could be dead. He was one of the most remarkable people I had ever known—a banker, Jewish by birth, Buddhist in his perspective, with a Catholic wife. In his remarkable life, he had developed a program for the United Nations to assist small house-hold industries in poor countries around the world. Later, he did the same on a larger scale for the Norwegian government, backed by the biggest bank in Norway. There was nothing in his manner or attitude, however, that could manifest his true stature. He had a humility that did not even appear as humility. I have been very blessed to have him as a part of my life. I passed on the news of Richard's passing in time for the dedication of the stupa in Louisville the next day, and his name was put forth at the consecration. Many there knew him. I continue to recall him daily, and that itself is a moment of prayer.

Before leaving for Asia, Richard asked me what I wanted him to bring back for me. I said I did not need anything, but added: "When you are in a sacred space, in a place of silence, think of me." He continued to do that

in his world travels. Now he is truly in a sacred place and
I fully expect him to remember me in the silence of his
new home.

With gratitude for the friends who deepen us,
Br. Paul

Dear Brother Paul,

I see from your letter about Shechen Rabjam Rinpoche
and the other Buddhist monks that the interfaith hospitality of Gethsemani, begun decades ago by your Father
Louis, is still bearing fruit. What an experience it must be
for you as a Western monk to pray with your Indian and
Tibetan guests.

I was particularly fascinated by the insight that came
to you at Mass that "every Christian is a reincarnation
of Christ." We are this reincarnation, as you say, because
we take in Christ present in the consecrated bread and
wine of the Mass. As I walk back to my pew after taking
Communion, I often reflect on the amazing fact that I am
carrying the body of Christ inside me. This thought is an
occasion for joy. At the same time, I feel convicted by all
of my faults. Who am I that my Lord should come to me?

After Mass ends, I usually try to take a few moments
to sit quietly in my pew and look at the large crucifix
above the altar. I gaze at the nails piercing the crucified
Christ, the wounded hands and feet, the protruding ribs,
the sagging head. It is a vision of agony, of pure pain.
Sometimes I imagine that my shortcomings—my anger,
egoism, and impatience—drive those nails more deeply

into Jesus' flesh, compounding his pain. It's my feeble attempt to keep the thought of inflicting pain on another with me to compel me to think before I act. So far, my grand scheme hasn't worked too well. I still fly off the handle. I still get impatient at times and let my ego carry me away.

But my time spent with the cross seems to have made me more aware now of how destructive those behaviors can be. Even if I can't seem to stop myself before I get angry or impatient, I'm quicker to apologize for my actions afterward. Perhaps I can take heart in such small progress.

I was also intrigued by your conversation about the notion of a fourth dimension of time that is not "the three"—past, present, and future—but includes St. Augustine's *toto simul,* everything in one instant. It reminded me of the late theologian John O'Donohue's idea of "unbroken presence," which encompasses the time before we are born, our time on earth, and the time after our death. O'Donohue says that the unbroken presence of our existence leaves an imprint "on the ether of a place, like secret tabernacles in a landscape." We exist in a triune vessel of past, present, and future. All is simultaneous.

When I worked for the *Wall Street Journal,* I wrote an article about a man named Paul Henderson, a well-known social worker who was dying of AIDS. I spent many months with Paul and his parents leading up to his death. Toward the end, Paul seemed to float in an in-between space between life and death. While bedridden, he began having visions of his parents, who were living with him at that time. He told of seeing them engaged in activities that had actually happened, but that he could not possibly have seen from the confinement of his bed. When I asked Paul about this, he said: "The line between life and death is thinner than you think." He was already living in some combined dimension of time and space.

It is all rather heartening to me—St. Augustine's concept of *toto simul,* O'Donohue's "unbroken presence," and Paul's dying declaration about the "thin line." It shows how the present rests on the stones of the past and that the future is already with us. So why worry? I don't mean to imply a defeatist attitude of predetermination that says every outcome is already sealed. I'm thinking of the Hindu priest in a *Passage to India* who declines to go on a journey because its unfortunate outcome has already been decided. The idea of time as a continuum of past, present, and future prompts me to think that what is meant to happen will eventually happen. Somehow, we will muddle through and all will be well in the end, as Julian of Norwich suggests.

Your letter also makes me reflect on the state of my own prayer life. I have never been very good at prayer. I'm probably one of the only people ever to flunk a retreat on "Prayer in Daily Life." I couldn't seem to carve out time for regular meetings with my spiritual director, much less time to write a prayer journal. This is why I love staying at monasteries. They offer distinct times for prayer, woven into the rhythm of the day. I remember walking with you outside the abbey church early one morning after Vigil prayers had ended. We stood there looking up at the planet Venus. There is something deeply humbling about interrupting your sleep to stand with others in prayer in the pre-dawn darkness. I felt a part of a mystery much larger than myself.

I do try to take short pauses in the course of my workday. It's my way of practicing a personal Liturgy of the Hours. I took this idea from Benedictine Sister Macrina Wiederkher's beautiful book, *Seven Sacred Pauses*. Our pauses can be as brief as stopping to observe a bird or a flower bed, she says, or as simple as breathing attentively. "Breathe in gratitude and compassion for yourself," she writes. "Breathe out love and encouragement for your coworkers, friends, family members . . . Your pause may be an awakening stretch or sitting quietly remembering your name."

Taking these brief pauses gives me a greater sense of having *lived* the day.

Yours in *toto simul*,
Judith

Dear Judith,

I encounter the same problem at Communion that you do. Perhaps I am expecting too much of myself. Perhaps I am too concerned about myself to be in a worthy state of mind, and so I seldom am. One of my spiritual directors said that it is presumptuous to think you could ever present a mind that is worthy to God. Perhaps it is enough to reconcile with the poverty of my state of mind and present that poverty to God.

One prayer method that helps me at Mass is to keep in mind the particular scripture readings of that day. I make a point of memorizing some part of the first reading and the Gospel. Then, during Mass, I reflect on how they interact. I "dog ear" each reading, the way you fold down a page in a book so you can return to it. I resist letting the reading go in one ear and out the other. So many of us forget what the readings were about as soon as Mass ends. Or worse yet, we can't recall what the reading was right after hearing it! If I retain and hold on to the readings, they become a context in which I can approach the altar and understand its mystery in the particular way presented by the specific readings of the day.

Alas, I often fail to do this and am left with a sense of personal vacuity. In this case, the best thing to do is not to think of anything, and to focus with an unoccupied mind—or better yet focus on silence, the silence about me, or the silence of a silent mind. That may be all the Lord expects and wants anyway.

I usually spend thirty or forty minutes after Mass in mindful meditation trying to stay present to the moment. This is one of the easiest, as well as hardest, practices, because I tend either to fall asleep or get restless. As I have learned from experience, I drift off because I am bored with my own mind. Meditation is not hard, as long as I do what I sat down to do, which is to stay present to the Presence. Then I can stay focused, or empty, or alert, or content with just being there.

Recently, there was a period of about two weeks when my meditation seemed dead. My spiritual director told me: "You don't know what is going on. Maybe that is the way the Lord wants it." Maybe Christ comes in his poverty and abandonment, and that is what I am experiencing as my own poverty. So it seems best just to let it alone, to take comfort in the faith that I just don't know what is going on.

I wrote a poem earlier this year named "Discontent" that bears upon this point:

> I step outside after Mass to my prayer nook
> with vague discontent.
> The clouded sky shows earlier light—
> the winter solstice seven days past—
> the temperature's milder, the air fragrant,
> birds are sounding,
> but none of this satisfies.
> I sit and hold on to discontent,
> indisposed for prayer,
> indisposed for anything else.
> After a while, my inability
> speaks from its poverty:
> Nothing within human capacity
> could ever be adequate for prayer.
> Truth alone is of any real worth.
> Let the truth of this moment, then,
> my discontent,
> be my prayer.

On December 10, the anniversary of Thomas Merton's death, a fellow monk quoted a passage of his that really speaks to the point here: "Christ always seeks the straw of the most desolate cribs to make his Bethlehem." I can dismiss this as self-comfort talk, or I can take it in faith as being true to everything I know of Christ. Even when meditation and quiet sitting seem to be of no evident worth, I know I would not want to be doing anything else. It is the only right thing for the time being.

I have little to complain about compared to the real poverty and desolation of so many poor people in the world today. My daily experience of singing the Liturgy of the Hours in chapel brings many moments of exaltation and joy. Just follow the music and the words and joy comes, especially at this time of year, in Advent. My prayers seem to be rejunvenated when Advent comes. A woman friend of mine calls it the season of the feminine. Think of Mary and Elizabeth's unexpected pregnancies, the Old Testament readings on Samson's mother, and Manoah's wife.

Tomorrow is the winter solstice, and we turn the corner to a new cosmic year. That is reflected in the O Antiphon for the day: "O Radiant Dawn! . . . Come give us light and warmth, for we sit in deep darkness, where we dwell in the shadow of death."

The solstice is especially significant for us at Gethsemani this year because it falls on the day in 1848 when the monks arrived here from France to establish a new monastery. The darkest day of the whole year! We will hear a reading about the monks' arrival during the first prayers of the morning and we will offer some other special prayers. The fact that our arrival in Kentucky happened at the time of the solstice gives me confidence—of what I am not sure. But look, here we are still. It is a sign that, in all their fears and hardships, those first monks perhaps "really did not know what was going on" except in hope.

The whole long story is bigger than our little piece in it.

Carry on,
Br. Paul

FRIENDSHIP

Dear Brother Paul,

There are many things about myself of which I am not proud. One thing in which I take pride, however, is being a good friend. I try to make my home a place of hospitality. But these past weeks have made me question whether I am a good and hospitable friend at all. And I am ashamed.

For the past three weeks, I have been entertaining a friend of mine from Paris and her husband. It is their first time visiting my home, and I wanted to make the visit a grand one. It ended up being a more complex and bitter-sweet experience than I could have imagined, however, full of nostalgia, sentiment, sadness, and regret.

I met A. when I was nineteen and studying at the Sorbonne during my junior year abroad. I arrived in Paris having lived a fairly sheltered life, ruled by strict, old-fashioned Italian-American parents. A. was two years older than I, already working, and, to my mind, far more sophisticated about fashion, the broader world, and the opposite sex. I was an aspiring writer even then and looked upon A. as a mentor. I think she also admired me for pursuing the kind of education she felt was closed to her under the rigid French university system.

Our friendship was intense, as friendships can be at that age. I imagined we were a feminine version of Charles Ryder and Sebastian Flyte in Evelyn Waugh's *Brideshead Revisited*—two people from different worlds whose lives intersect as university students and whose fates intertwine. When we saw the film *Julia*, the story of an aspiring novelist who takes life-threatening risks to save her friend—we walked out of the film saying: "That's us." It was not unusual back then for me to see the narrative of my life in all sorts of books and films. Such is the hubris of youth!

A.'s parents considered me a second daughter. Her father was a natural-born storyteller from Marseille— loud, gregarious, and often the center of attention, the antithesis of my own taciturn, unassuming father. Her mother was soft-hearted and gentle, in many ways the opposite of my own strong-willed, high-strung mother. I called them *Papa* and *Maman* and enjoyed many sumptuous meals around their table. Their apartment was in an elegant stone building near the Eiffel Tower, where guests were always welcomed with the warmest cordiality. In fact, I have always considered this family my gold standard for hospitality.

It was inevitable, I suppose, that A.'s life and mine would take different trajectories. She married in her twenties and had two children in quick succession. Even after her daughter and son were born, she continued to work at a bank. I went on to a career in journalism at the *Washington Post* and then the *Wall Street Journal*. I married much later in life and never had children. When I was still single, I got the impression that A. perceived my life as a free-flowing party, unfettered by commitments to a husband and children. I never expressed the loneliness I felt or the pressure I was under to perform at my peak at a large national newspaper.

I don't know what I was expecting from our reunion. I have many friends that I don't see on a regular basis, but I seem able to pick up with them as if no time at all has passed. You, Brother Paul, are one of them. I wanted to think that my decades-long friendship with A. would prove the same. But it quickly became obvious that we shared little in common anymore except the memories of our experiences from decades ago. In the ensuing years, we had become very different people, formed by the diverse paths each of us took. I wonder if memories from a distant past can prove sufficient to nurture an enduring friendship. I just don't know.

You once told me something that both fascinated and baffled me. You said you don't really *know* the other monks at the abbey. I found that astounding, since you have lived with some of them for more than sixty years! Perhaps friendship has a different meaning in a monastic context. Friends of mine who have been in religious life for a long time remember the days when superiors cautioned them against developing "particular friendships"—a warning, I suppose, against developing romantic or sexual feelings. I wonder if that mindset still exists and shadows relationships within religious communities even today.

You have often spoken with genuine affection of Thomas Merton, your spiritual adviser when you were a novice. But nothing of what you've ever told me or written suggests that you were friends with the man, that you actually knew or understood him in any deep way. Am I offbase on this?

You've gotten to know many of the regular guests at the monastery over the years, and many come to visit with you in particular. Do you consider them friends, or guests? My own sense is that friendship involves a deep and abiding devotion that can transcend frequent separations, geographic distance, and diverse life experiences. I would like to have that kind of friendship with A. Perhaps we must come to know each other as we are now, in midlife, and form new ties and new memories. Perhaps that's what the wise fox tries to teach the Little Prince in St. Exupery's story—that the meaning of friendship is "to create ties."

I look forward to hearing your thoughts on all this.

After A. and her husband left, I flew to Santa Barbara for a speaking engagement with an interfaith group that had selected my book *How to Live* for its "Word & Life" reading series. We had to leave for the airport at 3:00 AM for both the flight out to California and the flight back to Illinois. I kept thinking of you and the other Gethsemani monks, awake at that hour for Vigil prayers. The thought of the monks in the candlelit abbey church praying for our fragile world in the predawn hours filled me with comfort.

I thought too of what Merton wrote after one of his first visits to Gethsemani. "Now I know what has been holding the world together and keeping it from cracking into pieces. It is the prayers of this monastery."

In grateful friendship,
Judith

Dear Judith,

I was intrigued by your Merton quote. I'm of the opinion that monks who pray for the crazy world are exhibiting perhaps their own way of being crazy. When a woman asked a saintly Romanian monk what the first requirement was for becoming a monk, he answered: "You have to be crazy." I like my 3:00 AM way of being crazy.

Merton might subsequently have been embarrassed by his assessment of Gethsemani's prayers as "holding the world together." He made it in a youthful moment of exuberance. French Cistercian Charles Dumont has candidly pointed out that Merton can be "excessive" at times. One day when I was having spiritual direction with him, I held up "the golden mean"—the balancing point between extremes—as an ideal. He replied: "I believe in extremes." We laughed.

I cannot claim that I ever had a close friendship with Merton, or ever might have had. True, he knew me intimately as my spiritual director, but our relationship was not really a mutual friendship, any more than it was with his other novices. There were special moments, of course, like when his Undermaster left one can of beer on his desk for the Feast of St. Louis the King, his patron saint. Merton invited me into the office to share the can with him. We spent the time drawing sketches with felt-tip pens. I was impressed with his sketch of a lion's face and also his face of King David. (Both his parents were artists, as you know). I drew King David, but a slip of the pen gave him a drippy nose. Father Louis posted our creations on the bulletin board with a note saying that they were drawn by two Russian artists who had passed through the abbey that evening.

I think the capacity for friendship is elemental to spiritual development, as well as to human maturity. That does not mean that you have to claim a lot of friends; it means that the ability to handle intimacy is essential. I have a lot of friends; each one is different and each friendship involves different degrees of intimacy. Every relationship has its own perimeters and depths. You don't have to know everything about another person, or they about you. The right measure of friend-ship is whatever serves the Spirit and nourishes both people. In fact, friendship can be ruined by too much need for intimacy. That is where asceticism and the devel-opment of "skillful relationships" comes in. I am still in the process of learning about this and will remain so.

I have had my failures and my successes. When I make a friend, I do so intending to keep that person as a friend, but it does not always turn out that way. One of the hardest lessons to learn is that a relocation can carry a friend away forever. It is never *forever*, of course, since we will all meet again in eternity. But circumstances can be more determinative than I like to think. I now realize that this is part of being human. Circumstances determine when a friendship is formed, and circumstances can end it for all practical purposes.

All friendship is good while it lasts, but to cling to a relationship readily spoils it. Whether we like it or not, everyone has a life of their own to unfold, with duties and social obligations that take priority. I treasure what I have received from the many men and women I have known and, in the broader order of things, those relationships have their own fruitfulness and their own seasons, and are each pleasing to God. Perhaps your friend A. must count as one of these.

Friendships take on a different nature in a monastery. The monks are together day after day, and we come to know a lot about each other, despite our propensity for silence. Much of our communication takes place through gestures, expressions, and body movements. As for facts and details about the lives of other monks, I do not probe; and I am rarely questioned about my own life. The solitary atmosphere prevails. Much of our common understanding comes from having the same experiences and sharing the same history, the same training, and the same formation. Consequently, there is a lot that does not need to be explained.

One priest has shared monastic life with me since our early years. With him, I sometimes communicate about personal things, and vice-versa. This mutual confidence derives from our history and destiny. It does not thrive on chemistry so much as on a mutual love of our common life and the monastery. Having a common vocation facil- itates personal bonding, as well as bonding that is not particularly personal. By and large, that is the way it is for me with the other monks.

When I share no common vocation—as with my married and single friends—chemistry can get the relationship started. But those instinctual motivators fizzle out unless some mutual intellectual and spiritual interests prevail. In some cases, the very difference in our vocations creates interest. Mine is so unusual and unique that it attracts a strong interest from people outside of the monastery—not to mention that Gethsemani Abbey itself has its own unique mystique.

I find it helpful, however, to relate to people who are not surrounded by a mystique, who seem pretty ordinary. It keeps me normal and it awakens me to expressions of faith other than my own. As time goes by, I find deeper dimensions in each one of these outside friends, and a shared gratitude that we have remained in touch so long. That said, I also have several friends who are accomplished writers, poets, and musicians—friends who do come with a mystique of their own. You are one of them.

There is so much more that can be said about friendship. One of the best teachers is St. Aelred of Rievaulx, a Cistercian abbot of the 12th century. You could say there are different degrees of friendship. Some are based on mutual pleasure and some on mutual interests and concerns, where both parties are turned to the same object—a love shared together. But friendship in the strict sense, as I see it, is a face-to-face relationship, one in which I am interested in you for your own sake and you are interested in me for my own sake. Without this mutuality, there is no friendship in the fullest sense. Ultimate friendship is not about what others have or how they look. It's not about how others can please me. It is a pure, disinterested desire that others be who they are meant to be, and an abiding love even if they fail.

In effect, that is the kind of love that God has for me. The more I can experience that divine love, the more capable I become of loving others in the same way. A really human love is sustainable through all the stresses a friendship may face—even in the face of death, departure, or separation. Thus prayer proves to be the matrix of friendship that carries me beyond my own capacities.

To that extent, friendship is more than my love for others. It is love loving *in me*. To modify St. Paul's words: "I love, now not I, but Love loves in me." I often feel deficient in love, and sometimes pray that I may become loving. But that is already love prodding me on to be more of what it is in me—more of what I am meant to be in the fullest sense. For this I have not lost hope.

May your hope be the same in this one love,
Br. Paul

NAVIGATING THE UNEXPECTED

Dear Judith,

I had a dream about you last night—about us, really. We were going to participate in some conferences for women in the abbey's Retreat House. But when I looked at your You Tube site, one of the side frames indicated you were ill and under the care of a doctor. The next day, however, you arrived at the retreat well and whole. In the dream, many women had gathered for the retreat, but I had made no preparation and did not know what I would talk about. Then an alarm went off and there I was, totally alone.

The dream, surprisingly, prepared me for today's reading from John's gospel that says: "You do not know where the Spirit comes from or where it goes." The only qualification given is that it comes "from above" (*anothen*) and goes one knows not where. I like that note of total openness. It indicates a mind free of any prede-termination. In the open is where we start and that is where we go. Or maybe there is no coming and no going, just standing under the sky and being open to what happens moment by moment. Life is too plentiful to be limited by our narrow expectations. Wait and watch, and it will show itself in many forms—as it did this morning when I awoke and the clouds took on color and the birds crossed my sight.

In this openness, I wait, and what emerges is a gift of the openness. This happens if I am still and attentive. It does not ask me for attention, but I offer it and am rewarded. Every day in openness can be something of a gift, and sufficient for the day are the gifts thereof and the troubles. If I meet the troubles as well as the gifts with the same openness, they are not absolute. They are of the day. If the troubles are really big and change the course of my life, this is a new call upon my freedom—my freedom to say "yes" or to set my sails on a different tack, since that is where the wind blows.

In our uncertain world, some will sink or watch a loved one perish. Real awareness requires us to know that we are all sailing on the same sea. What the sea is today for others it may be tomorrow for me. That is part of the common "openness," the actual condition of life that is ours to be in from day to day.

What matters is that we not try to explain what happens, that we not ignore it or wish that it were all different. What is, is what it is. I need a day like today to see life for what it is; to shift my gaze from the immediate track of work and routine, to take position on what the

wind and the sky are bringing. Can you be ready for that?
Can I be ready for that?

> Let us be true to life, and ready,
> Br. Paul

Dear Brother Paul,

Your recent dream about me is more prescient perhaps
than you can imagine. I was particularly struck by these
words: "What matters is that we not try to explain what
happens, that we not ignore it or wish that it were all
different."

This is a letter I have put off writing, because I
couldn't seem to find the right words or where to start.
Perhaps I should begin by telling it "slant," as our poet
guide Emily Dickinson was fond of saying. A friend
invited me to her yoga class the other day and this is the
passage the instructor read as a closing meditation: "I
must have wandered upon this path for a reason. Maybe
it was a quick reminder to catch my breath." *I must have
wandered upon this path for a reason.*

Let me start with the Friday afternoon that my husband told me that an oncologist's office had called earlier
in the day and wanted to speak with me about making
an appointment. Earlier in the month, I had had a needle
biopsy to investigate some suspicious tissue in my left
breast. Not welcome news, but I had been through this
once before several years ago and the results turned out
to be normal. Now the results of the biopsy were in. I

didn't call the oncologist, but rather a neighbor who happens to be a nurse in my GP's office. She told me that the biopsy results showed cancer in one of the ducts of my left breast.

I couldn't believe what I was hearing. It made no sense. I rarely take so much as an aspirin. I eat a largely Mediterranean diet; I exercise five times a week. How is this happening to *me*? And why is it happening *now*, when I have speaking engagements, retreats to guide, an upcoming book tour in Australia, and a new book to write? I kept thinking that no one besides my husband could know about this. I feared that, if my publisher found out, I wouldn't get another book contract, or my editors would think I couldn't finish the book I was working on. I began thinking that the letters c-a-n-c-e-r spelled only one thing: demise.

Two days later, a nurse practitioner in my GP's office informed me that the cancer appeared to be *in situ*, meaning it hadn't spread. That was supposed to be a good thing. She went on to say that my cancer was considered a "level zero to one," so no chemotherapy would be necessary, but I had to undergo surgery and then several weeks of radiation treatment. I told her I didn't have time for surgery or radiation, that I had presentations to give, retreats to lead, etc, etc. The nurse gave me a referral to a surgeon and said: "People will understand." I only wished that *I* could "understand."

On the ride home, I kept thinking about how I'm the youngest sibling in my family. I'm not supposed to die first. Then I remembered that the youngest siblings of both my mother and my father had been the first to die—one of a brain tumor and the other of breast cancer. Later, a friend of mine who is a surgeon told me that, if you have to have breast cancer, a diagnosis of noninvasive ductal cancer is the best kind to have. His encouragement doesn't help me sleep at night.

To be continued,
Judith

Dear Brother Paul,

Writing to give you an update. I've now been to see the surgeon and we had a rather cordial discussion about my case. But when I asked about a clinical study in which patients with my form of breast cancer are being treated with medication alone, she informed me rather sternly that she provided only "standard of care" treatment—surgery followed by radiation. Period. End of conversation.

I guess she could sense my negative reaction, because she observed that I "seemed angry" about my diagnosis. Not angry, I said, just mystified—puzzled that this would be happening now, out of the blue, without my experiencing any overt symptoms. I likened it to walking down a street minding my own business and suddenly being hit on the head by a falling brick. What I didn't want to say is that this diagnosis doesn't fit my image of myself as invincible. I'm the person the family looks to when things need to get done. Friends ask *me* to pray for *them*, not the other way around.

Merton said we walk around most of the time being the person we think others believe we are, and miss experiencing our true selves. Perhaps this diagnosis is at long last tugging me away from the false self I've cultivated and dragging me toward the true.

I thanked the surgeon for her time. Then I went home and asked my nurse practitioner for a referral to Mayo Clinic.

Still hoping for a better outcome,
and maybe finding my true self,
Judith

Dear Brother Paul,

We arrived at the Mayo Clinic yesterday for a round of tests. For such a high-tech medical center, the Mayo still manages to feel—how should I put it?—oddly personal. A pianist plays in the lobby of the building where most patients arrive, and the various treatment and research buildings are decorated with art from around the globe—from paintings to fabrics to ceramics. Amid much illness, there is also much beauty.

Just before we left home, I received an email from Mayo saying that I wouldn't be seeing the specialist I was originally assigned, but another doctor. All of the best doctors I've ever known are ones I have met by accident, so I found this last-minute change somewhat comforting. And this time proved no different. I *love* my doctor. Her first words to me were: "I have good news for you." It seems that I *don't* have ductal breast cancer after all; I have something called "atypical hyperplasia." Although I didn't know what that meant, the operative words for me were: "You don't have breast cancer." Then I heard more welcome words: "No radiation." I will still likely have to have surgery to remove these atypical cells, because, if left undisturbed, they may increase my chance of developing breast cancer in the future.

I wasn't thrilled when I heard that I had to have an MRI, however. I get claustrophobic just entering a closet. But my doctor prescribed an anti-anxiety pill for me to take before the test and a friend of mine told me that she got through MRIs by imagining that the loud banging sound made by the machine was Native American drumming. As it turned out, the experience was a lot less stressful than I had imagined. I'm glad, because I'll need to get an MRI once a year from now on.

I realize that I haven't yet told you very much about how this whole experience has affected my spiritual life. I really haven't had a lot of time to reflect on it. I've been so focused on my body that I haven't had any energy left to consider what is happening to my spirit. It's as if my body has become an extension of all the technology and equipment that has geared up to keep me healthy.

I don't want people worrying about me, so I haven't asked my friends, or even the sisters at the monastery where I'm an Oblate, for prayers. I've only told a handful of people about the diagnosis. I suppose that's part of not wanting my vulnerability laid bare. When I pray, it is for the other women I see in the breast center waiting rooms, who all seem similarly determined to keep to themselves, although we are all there for the same tests. Collectively, we hope for good news. I know there are women in those rooms facing far more serious diagnoses than mine. I pray for them, not for myself.

As I look back on the Mass readings from the past month or so, it is odd how many passages seem to have foreshadowed what I was about to experience. From the gospel of Matthew, Jesus traveling "around all of Galilee . . . curing every illness and disease." From Mark, Jesus walking on the sea, exhorting the apostles to "take courage . . . Be not afraid!" and healing a leper and a paralytic. And from Psalm 107: "They cried to the Lord in their need/ and God rescued them in their distress/ sending forth a word to heal them/ saving their life from destruction."

Just before Christmas, I attended a "Tree of Hope" lighting ceremony at our Community Cancer Center. A woman I know only slightly from my fitness class had been asked to light the tree and say a few words about her cancer experience. I don't even think I had previously known this woman's first name, but as she and I chatted that evening, she told me that one of the surprising things about her experience was that friends she thought would be there to support her, weren't. Those who stepped up were people whom she wouldn't have expected to do so. As if to prove her point, this relative stranger has become one of the people to whom I now turn for advice and support. Although her diagnosis was far more serious than mine, she has remained unceasingly optimistic.

While visiting with a friend who is a Presbyterian minister, a poet, and a mother with two sons in college and a daughter in high school, I let slip something about what I was going through. Now, despite her busy life, she pops over to the house with bags of groceries so I don't have to worry about shopping. She drops off a basil plant or some boxes of tea. Before she leaves, she usually asks if we can pray together. And we do. Even my religion-skeptic husband joins in.

In a health crisis, the smallest things take on outsized significance. My fitness instructor sent me off to Mayo with a tiny pink blanket from the American Cancer Society. I kept it with me through all the tests and consults. My friends from Italy sent me a photo of my favorite church, La Madonna del Carmine, in their town of Guardiagrele. When I look at the photo, I imagine I am in the pews looking up at the Madonna. That is perhaps the closest I come to praying for myself. All these friends are like the "invisible hands" that mythologist Joseph Campbell talks about—hands that arrive seemingly from nowhere to help you on your way.

Has my outlook on life changed? I don't really know yet. I'm still processing the whole experience and will leave that perhaps for a future letter. I keep thinking of something Merton once told a monk who was considering leaving the monastic community: "Relax and live." A lesson I am still learning.

Relaxing for now, and still living,
Judith

Dear Judith,

I appreciate your honesty in sharing your scare over "the c-word." My dad died of cancer when I was ten years old. He was ill for only a few brief months, but all the hope, prayers, anticipation, and disappointments made it seem as if his illness went on forever. Somehow, I knew even then that, just because I prayed for my Dad not to die, that didn't mean he wouldn't. Up to the end, Mother never said my father would die. But she wouldn't say he wouldn't die either. I was given a special grace to know that there was no other likely outcome for him with the kind of cancer he had. I think that helped ease the blow when his time came.

Of course, in my larger monastic "family," there have been many cancer deaths. The most touching was that of a brother who died of lung cancer in 1970 at the age of thirty. After growing up in a Protestant family, he converted to Catholicism and entered the monastery as a lay brother at a young age, at approximately the same time I did. He is one of the monks I don't hesitate to call "saintly." He seemed to harbor no hostilities and was the soul of innocence. He appeared resigned to his diagnosis when it came and continued to work as the monastery's electrician, even when he was supposed to be confined to bed.

Brother Rene, who lived a similarly exemplary life, approached his illness differently. He fought for his life to the end. His esophagus required radiation, and it became impossible for him to swallow and to eat. He suffered a great deal of pain and it seemed crazy to me for him to continue treatment, but that is what he wanted. Yet another monk lived three years beyond what doctors expected. He had many projects he wanted to finish up and he loved the work.

I have noticed that monks tend to die the way they lived. Those with slower temperaments die slowly; those with quicker temperaments, like Merton, die quickly. Lovers of liturgy tend to die liturgically—like Abbot James Fox, who died on Good Friday. Our liturgist passed away in bed as the consecration was taking place at Mass. I like to say that my preferred manner of death would be to go alone into the woods and crawl under some leaves so that they will not find me until someone notices a swarm of buzzards circling over the spot.

Perhaps life does us a favor when it blindsides us with a crisis. Perhaps it does this just to remind us that we are not in total control. I am not sure that this always brings us an awareness of the *true* self; but it certainly does bring us to the *real* self, with all its limitations.

The life we can control is real as well, of course. But it is not the whole of life, although we are easily caught up in it. In a way, illness can make us too preoccupied with self-concern, and that becomes a big spiritual challenge. Your way of praying for others who are worse off than you—that is a healthy response. Suffering can, at best, open us to empathy, to awareness, and to participation in the vast suffering of countless others in the world. I hope that, if I ever must bear such misfortunes, I will come to such an inclusive empathy.

Yours in understanding,
Br. Paul

MEDITATION

Dear Brother Paul,

I don't know how the weather has been in northern Kentucky, but here in central Illinois, we are experiencing a mini monsoon season. Sometimes the heavy gray clouds feel like an oppression, like stones on my shoulders. What is it that Merton wrote in *New Seeds of Contemplation*? "The special clumsy beauty of this particular colt on this April day in this field under these clouds is a holiness consecrated to God . . . and it declares the glory of God." I suppose the desolate clouds and wild rain participate in their own kind of holiness. They seem perfectly satisfied with what they are, and that is perhaps both their glory and their wisdom.

Thank you for your thoughtful letter. I had forgotten that your father died of cancer. Your observations on how various monks died is both fascinating and curious. I suppose it is only natural that some will resign themselves to whatever happens, and that others will fight to the end. Much to your chagrin, I fear, I will probably be one of those who decides to "rage, rage against the dying of the light."

I remember Brother Rene. He left quite a profound impression on me. One evening, I happened to be in the abbey's meditation chapel when he came in to lead a recitation of the rosary. I hadn't planned to stay, but since no one else showed up, I remained. He mentioned that he would soon be going to a hospital in Louisville for treatment. Every time he finished saying a decade of Hail Marys, he paused to say a short prayer of his own. He prayed for peace in the world, for unity in families, for the poor, for the lonely. But not once did he pray for himself, for his own healing. His attentiveness to the needs of others rather than his own has remained with me. A few weeks later, you told me he had died.

Since I returned from Mayo, I have been studying meditation with a Tibetan Lama named Tsering Ngodup Yodsampa. I have also been rereading Merton's writings on contemplative prayer. Even when he was still in his solidly Catholic apologetic phase, before he began exploring Buddhist monasticism and mysticism, Merton was writing about prayer in a way that sounds a lot like Buddhist meditation. He found the deepest form of prayer in silence.

As you know, I have been attending daily Mass for quite a while now and I'm finding the wordiness of the liturgy increasingly irritating—all those elaborate Collects and Eucharistic prayers that contain a riot of words and archaic expressions. It's as if they are composed by the same people who write the fine-print warnings on consumer products. I feel as if I have to trudge through a forest of verbiage before the simple clarity of "This is my body . . . This is my blood . . . do this in remembrance of me" breaks through. Perhaps these are the only truly necessary words of the Mass.

Merton tried to dispense with useless verbiage. He describes God as mystery, as darkness, as pure truth, as the ground of our being whom we know by unknowing—or, as he says: "We know *beyond* all knowing or unknowing." God is beyond words, he writes in *New Seeds of Contemplation,* yet "speaks in everything that is, and who most of all speaks in the depths of our own being, for we are words of his."

We are words of his. This is the understanding of God I intuit in listening to Lama Tsering. He may refer to "the Buddha within," but what I think he means is that spark in each of us that is free from illusion and attachment, that is the seed of God within. He calls meditation a mental collaboration with our physical breathing, something that reminds me of what Merton said in his essay "Day of a Stranger": "What I wear is pants, what I do is live, how I pray is breathe."

How I pray is breathe. Easy, right? Hard for me. Lama Tsering often compares the mind to a racehorse that can carry us into a thicket of thoughts during meditation. If my mind were a racehorse, it could probably run the Kentucky Derby, the Preakness, and the Belmont Stakes all in the same meditation session. I've finally gotten the meditation posture down pat, but I can't seem to keep my mind from galloping from one thought to the next. I can usually return my focus to my breathing—for all of about ten seconds. Then the starter pistol sounds and I burst out of the gate again.

I wonder if you experience some of the same struggles in your own meditation practice. Or does the practice improve over time? Even in my compromised meditative state, I still come away from these prayer sessions feeling as if something has shifted inside of me. I feel a little less attached to particular outcomes and have a greater sense of the interdependence of things. Lama Tsering never talks exclusively about human beings, but rather about "all sentient beings." It's a recognition, I suppose, that humans are but one link in the chain of beings. This morning as I was writing this letter, a moth kept flying near my computer screen. I *hate* having any kind of flying, crawling, creeping insects near me. But as I was about to grab the moth and squash it, I stopped. I cupped it loosely in my hands and politely escorted it, still alive, out our front door. I felt I owed this moth as much as a fellow sentient being. I trust it will be happier outside.

My favorite part of these prayer sessions is when we recite the prayer for compassion, well-being, and long life—*Om tare tuttare ture soha*—although I've yet to find a good translation of the words. I don't really need to know their exact meaning. I just love the way the syllables sound. It's enough to know that, when I pronounce them, I'm engaging in an ancient practice for seeking release, not only from physical suffering, but from the suffering that comes from my pride, delusion, anger, ignorance, jealousy, greed, and desire. As I sound the words, I am praying for "all sentient beings."

When my friend, poet Lisa Breger, was a lymphoma patient in Boston, the Lama chanted the *Om tare tuttare ture soha* prayer whenever he visited her. She ultimately survived her bone marrow treatments and became well again. She doesn't claim that the prayer magically cured her lymphoma. But she does say that the prayer brought her peace.

Your mindfully racing friend,
Judith

Dear Mindfully Racing Judith,

I think my problems at meditation are almost opposite to yours. I tend to plunge into sleep. I start out with good posture and attentiveness. But, before I am aware of it, I have fuzzed into an opaque slump. This often starts with thoughts that seem to be leading somewhere and tease me to follow. But they lead nowhere. When I come to, I can hardly account for what I was thinking.

Thinking itself seems to spiral downward, even when it appears justified. That is because meditation is not a time for thinking; it is a time for simple awareness. Occasionally, if I review what is going through my mind, that helps me leave thought behind and recover awareness. Simple awareness of the present.

Paradoxically, that much simplicity and focused stillness sometimes proves more than I can handle, although I resist admitting that to myself. I have an affinity for complexity, not to mention excitement and distraction. Nevertheless, I must bear simplicity, abide it, stay the time, devote myself more, judge it not, and trust to the commitment—faltering as it may be.

I recently read something written by American Buddhist nun Pema Chödrön in which she says we should not meditate with any expectation that we will eventually get better at it. Likewise, we mustn't expect to become better people, or more enlightened people. How liberating that is! And how true to my long experience. I'm no better at meditation after sixty-plus years in the monastery, it appears to me, than I ever was. In fact, meditation seems to have become more insufferable and drier to me, to the point where I have taken to oral prayer in which I recite psalms or poems or hymns that I have memorized.

That is a relief, and one that the Desert Fathers would have appreciated, since they frequently turned over the same scripture line or passage in their minds throughout the day. Some recited the entire Psalter every day as a form of interior work. Work, manual labor in particular, was their remedy to *acedia*—boredom and dryness. I do manual labor every day in the kitchen or elsewhere, so I find this more interior labor helpful, especially if it is as simple as saying: "Lord, Jesus Christ, have mercy on us." That, in effect, is like the Desert Fathers' simple work of weaving baskets or us making and boxing our fudge. Both free the soul for prayer. When idle, I can become burdened with myself—weighed down with guilt, frustration, disappointment, self-dissatisfaction, and subjective static that leads nowhere.

This, however, is only part of the problem. There is something more radical at play than this—something that has to do with the human condition, with my own existence as one and only, as a finite being in this world. The feeling shows itself when I allow myself the awareness that I exist on the threshold of the unlimited, the absolute, the transcendent. I may not express it to myself in those terms (better not to), but the idea imposes itself in wordless meditation. It is simply there as a very condition of existence.

Meditation is a moment to abide with that sense of being on the threshold of the limitless, a moment that can become habitual through a regular meditation practice. But for all that, how much of this consciousness can we abide? We necessarily feel incommensurate to it; we feel it mostly unconsciously. But there it is. A 14th-century author spoke of it as "the cloud of unknowing." He speaks of desire as piercing the cloud—an absurd image, since you cannot pierce a cloud. But love attempts anything, I guess. Whether you are actively sending those darts of love or not, the cloud is there. It is part of the human condition in the face of the great mystery.

When I get realistic, I accept abiding at this point of helplessness, and that is when I am ready for help. Grace can then make an entrance. That is the moment of mercy, a moment to realize that, ultimately, it is not all up to me. I can relax and allow existence to be as it is. That realization does not necessarily come while we are self-aware, when we have a sense of being a subject and a recipient. Better just to let it happen as and when it is happening.

As I get further along in life, I suspect that what is required is a lifelong abiding on "the threshold" before the full reality comes—a reality we do not perceive. That is why humility is elemental. The core humility I am destined for in life is my seeming lack of fulfillment itself. Such humility is not something you "have"; it is the helpless sense that you have nothing of your own, not even humility. That's just the way life is. It is your life and just the way you are given to be.

I cannot make humility another object of *care*, try as I may. I mean the self-referential effort to be humble. Real humility, according to one Cistercian Father, does not know it is a virtue. Instead, it is a matter of *being*, however you may be, ignorant of anything beyond simply being.

This morning, I stumbled across a quotation from volume 7 of Merton's personal journals that suggests where this is all going: "I am the utter poverty of God. I am [God's] emptiness, littleness, nothingness, lostness. When this is understood, my life is [God's] freedom, the self-emptying of God in me, the fullness of grace" (May 16, 1968).

A lot of this reflection is perhaps coming from the fact that I have been living under a gray featureless sky for a few days now in which the clouds are not even dramatic and gloomy. Just flat.

Your mindfully slouching one,
Br. Paul

LIVING WITH THE UNIMAGINABLE

Dear Judith,

Well what seemed impossible has happened. Americans must hunker down and stay in place. In short, they are now living more like monks. It will be interesting to see what results come from this new way of life that has been forced on us by the corona-virus pandemic. One thing is certain; life will change, for better or for worse. I suspect some people will not know what to do with themselves. Some will drink or seek recreation in drugs. I can only imagine what the birth rate will be nine months from now!

On the other hand, others will use this time to accomplish what they have longed to do, but were too busy to *C'est moi* complete—read a backlog of books, fix up the house, go quietly into a more contemplative state of mind, perhaps even pray.

At our abbey, the retreat house is now closed to the public, as is the gift shop and the church. Our hired workers have been put on a subsidy rather than receiving their usual pay, and attend only to work that is necessary.

The monks continue to celebrate Mass and chant the Liturgy of the Hours. In the part of our church where we have choir stalls and gather for communal prayer, we keep vacant places between monks. We also leave empty seats between us in the area where we celebrate Mass. The funny thing is that, with all this separation, our singing sounds better. People sing out more loudly and it is easier to hear the organ, so the pitch is better. We may never go back to standing side by side!

We know from our annual bouts of flu how quickly illness spreads around the monastery. If COVID-19 sneaks in, things could get very bad very quickly. This virus is smart; it creeps up and gestates for two weeks before you know you have it. My peculiar fantasy is to test as a carrier without the symptoms. Then I could quarantine myself in my office like a hermit. It would be a little like the solitary week I am allowed each summer at the Merton hermitage, but my office "hermitage" would have a phone, a computer, and web access. I suppose it would be a pretty questionable site in which to live a hermit's life in the final analysis.

I was recently asked by CNN to give a monastic point of view on the COVID-19 crisis. I was inspired to write the following:

> I think this epidemic brings with it the chance for
> positive change. It makes us feel our vulnerability
> and take seriously our real values and priorities.
> Suddenly people are having to stay at home and
> move more slowly and quietly. This could well be

the most difficult part of the pandemic for many.
As Blaise Pascal said: "Man's unhappiness springs
from one thing alone, his incapacity to stay qui-
etly in one room."

I see the current situation as an opportunity. It is a time when people can get to know themselves better, grow closer to their families, and spend more time reading, listening. It is a chance to get over the fear of solitude and to find actual comfort in life that transcends scurrying from this to that. You must return to yourself to find that which transcends yourself, however you name it.

Preoccupations can crop up, even in a monastery, but the structure prescribed by our monastic day weighs against them. Learning to structure our free time is an important discipline. It makes the passing of the hours more tolerable and makes staying quiet easier. When I spend a week alone at the Merton hermitage, I make a point of observing the appointed times spaced throughout the day for praying the Psalms in the Liturgy of the Hours. I read and write during the other hours and spend some time just doing nothing, like sitting on the porch and watching shadows grow across the lawn. In all this apparent emptiness, there is the sense of presence of what cannot be spoken. I am never less alone than when alone, as St. Bernard used to say (and Cicero before him). Call it faith if you will, or not. If you let it happen, it will happen.

Beyond all that, this epidemic is an opportunity to develop empathy. We have run short on our supply of empathy and compassion, and suddenly we are made to face our common humanity. Awareness of how we are one—especially in our fragility—is the ground from which we build community. A life driven by desire to prove yourself better than others, to leave others behind, and to stand out is a life of forgetfulness. We mostly live in a swamp of forgetfulness that eventually drains away our humanity. Now is the time for that to stop.

One of the best things to learn and learn again is the simple joy of being together. Love starts at home, as we find ways to pass time by engaging as families in creative leisure and play. For unloving families, this may turn out to be a terribly hard time that may demand learning another way of being. For others, it will be the life they have long wanted, but for which they never had enough time. School is now out for all intents and purposes; businesses are shut down. But perhaps now a different kind of education can begin, along with the real business of life, which is to learn to live.

I, for one, thank heaven for these times, terrible as they are. They can make us more genuine as human beings, more cooperative as a country, more united as a world. It is surely a legendary time. When it is all over, many of us will have a story to tell. Sadly, however, some will not live to tell theirs. It will be for the living to pass on the stories of those lives.

> May you stay healthy and strong as
> we both await the next chapter,
> Br. Paul

Dear Brother Paul,

What a surreal time!

Just three weeks ago, I was rejoicing at being told I don't have cancer. I was wandering through garden centers, selecting vegetables to plant in my backyard, planning the menu for the Easter brunch I host every year at my home, attending my daily fitness classes. Now I wear a face mask and surgical gloves to do the grocery shopping. My husband and I have stopped traveling and receive no guests (very unusual for our home). Hardly anyone passes by our house on the street. We try to take a short walk once a day, careful to keep the prescribed six feet of distance should we encounter anyone. That is how much life has changed within a matter of days. It is like being a character in an episode of the *Twilight Zone*.

For you and I and other monkish writer types, the crisis has caused only a slight variation to our work routines. "Social distancing" and "sheltering in place," phrases that have newly entered the national lexicon, really aren't unfamiliar ways of being for writers. I've been gone for over a year now from my job in daily journalism, so I no longer have the habit of going into an office every day and interacting with the public. I am very much a "people person," but I also recognize that solitude is essential in order to write.

My husband is finding it much harder to stay close to home. I wouldn't be exaggerating if I told you that, every couple of hours, he asks if I need him to run out to the grocery store. He looks crestfallen if my answer is "no."

The truth is, I want him going into stores as infrequently as possible. Whoever thought grocery shopping could become a life-threatening endeavor? He passes the time binge-watching shows on TV. It's probably ruining his eyes, not to mention his posture, but if this offers some respite from boredom, it's alright with me. Frankly, I wish he would work on our tax filing instead, but I'm loathe to nag him under such conditions.

I really don't mean to make light of this situation. The stay-at-home orders have put millions of people out of work and made it impossible for them to put food on the table. My heart aches for them. We've tried to support our local food bank and international aid groups. If, however, we stay focused on the tragedy of it all, we just might go crazy.

Sometimes I burst into tears watching people on the news describe how they couldn't be with family members when they died because of the hospital restrictions in place. I can empathize with the pain this causes, because each time one of my parents died, I was living in another city. It haunts me to this day that I was not able to be with them in their final moments. I shudder to imagine what it is like for those who die of the virus on ventilators, alone in hospital rooms.

I can almost hear your voice saying: "Yes, but we all die alone. We can't send a substitute." I guess the point is that it would have meant something to me—and to those others—to have been present for our loved ones, to write that last sentence, to give that final goodbye.

At the start of the crisis, when it seemed as if we all might well succumb to the virus, I began to question the choices I've made over the course of my life. Were all those years I worked in journalism a waste? Should I have written more poetry? Will I have time to write another collection of poems? Do I have another spirituality book in me? Why did I wait so long to marry? The one question that haunts me most is probably the most difficult one: Did I love enough?

Certainly, these fifteen years with my husband have been a constant outpouring of love. I don't regret a minute of it, even the stupid, unnecessary arguments that inevitably arise in any marriage. What troubles me is all those other years before I married, when my journalism career was my consuming passion. I placed work above relationships, neglected people who needed my attention. I can identify with the character in the film *Photograph*, who says: "I wish that I was as good at love as I am at working. I wish I didn't leave people behind so often."

Something unexpected happened in the midst of this review of my life. I received a call from a young man who is writing a biography of one of my first editors at the *Washington Post*. This particular editor was a brilliant, immensely talented man who died of AIDS when he was only forty-five. The young man who called me wanted to know about the atmosphere at the *Post* during the years I worked there. He had researched articles I had written during my seven years with the paper, most of which I'd forgotten over the years. He observed that so many of the articles were about people on the margins, people whose voices were ignored by the larger society.

I often tell young reporters that the most important trait a reporter can develop is compassion. It's more important than writing or interviewing skills, or even having knowledge of a particular subject. You have to care about the people you write about. They feel it when you do and sense it when you don't. Talking with that young writer reminded me of how much I had cared about the people I interviewed as a journalist. Dare I say, I even loved them? That may sound like an endorsement for biased journalism. I guess what I mean is that perhaps that was how I loved in those days. Through my work. Was it enough? I don't know.

Certainly the threat of contracting a deadly illness has lit a fire under me to finish my writing projects, because who among us knows the day or the hour? At the same time, I've become more willing to put people ahead of my work. When friends looking for some form of human contact call, text, or email, I answer. I don't get frustrated by the interruption. I don't rush to end the phone call. Some days, it takes me hours to respond to all the calls and messages.

The stay-at-home directives are particularly difficult for people who live alone. You, Brother Paul, have your community of monks. I have my husband. I think back to the many years when I was single, living on my own in a studio apartment. If I had to live that way under these current conditions, I'd feel like the caged animal in Rainer Maria Rilke's poem "The Panther," whose vision "grows weary" from pacing and whose will "stands paralyzed."

The forced isolation has caused me to notice what's been right in front of me all along that I failed to see. I'm filled with a new appreciation for our mail carrier, who every day risks touching letters and packages smeared with God knows how many germs. Whenever I see a neighbor pass the house (a rare occurrence these days), I tap on the window and wave. I am grateful for the chatty checkout clerk at the supermarket. I notice the men and women stocking the shelves or working in the deli and the bakery, putting themselves at risk so I can bring home food to eat. I think of my neighbor, who is a nurse, and my friend's son, who is a doctor, both serving the sick. I'm grateful for the workers at our local pharmacy. I will never *not* see them again.

I try to send a text every day to our friends and family in Italy. Italians love to parade in the streets, parks, and piazzas, but now they can't even go out for a stroll. They need a permission slip just to go to the grocery store. And in the midst of it, they show the world how to confront this crisis, not only with courage, but with beauty and grace. Neighbors serenade each other from their balconies. To lift their patients' spirits, doctors and nurses in overcrowded infection wards play the national anthem over a loudspeaker. My friends sent me a photo of two Capuchin priests carrying the Blessed Sacrament in a monstrance through their neighborhood, blessing houses as they went. I read an account of a Polish priest assigned to the Vatican who has been delivering food to the homeless. He told seminarians studying in Rome: "Put away the theology books for now. There is a gospel in the making on the streets." Sure enough. Would that I could have his brand of courage.

A line from one of my favorite films from the Eighties, *The Year of Living Dangerously*, seems appropriate for this time. Let us "do what we can about the misery right in front of us. And by doing so, add light to the sum of light."

Here's hoping that we both
can add to the sum of light,
Judith

Dear Brother Paul,

Today the country passed a grim milestone: the highest number of corona virus deaths in a single day. I walked around grief-stricken for much of the day. Then the Super Moon rose.

The moon shone brighter and larger than it will on any other night this year, shedding a light that was a cross between amber and rose. Earlier in the day, a friend sent me a photo of a tiny yellow wildflower inching its way out of some dry soil. "This small flower has been popping up near my brother's house each spring for over forty years," he wrote. "I have no idea what it is, but it is the color of hope to me now." Last night's brilliant moon and that small, persistent flower (perhaps a tiny mum) forced me to look beyond the current darkness. True, the world is experiencing a dangerous and uncertain time, but the universe rolls on. It does what it does, which is to lean into life.

Here in Illinois, redbuds are blooming and lilac bushes are beginning to sprout green shoots. Cream-colored jonquils shoot up overnight, bowing their blossom heads like hooded monks at prayer. Between blades of grass, violets spread a carpet of color. No one told them it was their time to emerge. No one controls their arrival. It is as if, amid so much death, creation won't stop shouting of life.

My Jewish friends say that it will be a Passover like no other, with families joining the *seder* table, not in person, but virtually, online. This year when they commemorate the tenth plague—the deaths of Egyptian firstborns—and keep an eye on the door for the appearance of Elijah, they will be on guard as well for signs of a modern plague. Unlike the one in Exodus, however, this one doesn't discriminate between Jew and Gentile. It is an equal-opportunity slayer of innocents. When our friends recite the prayers recalling the Israelites' release from slavery, they will be praying for freedom from a microscopic scourge as well.

As Holy Week approaches, many people will experience a personal Passion. Intensive care units are our contemporary Calvarys. In the Passion story, women come to bury Jesus. Joseph of Arimethea donates a tomb. In cities across the U. S., coffins pile up in front of funeral homes. Who will bury our dead? In their silence, the moon and spring flowers may seem indifferent, but by their presence, they speak of hope. They point to a resurrection beyond the current suffering.

You and the monks at the abbey will be among the few to celebrate Easter in a physical church this year. With churches closed, the rest of us will have to attend a virtual service or, like me, worship in the open-air church of creation, beneath sky and trees. Not going to a traditional church this Easter is fine with me. I can do without yet another uninspired homily on the Resurrection, an event so inexplicable that it can only be understood in the crucible of the heart. I've been thinking of the root word for "church" and its grounding in the Latin *ecclesia* and the Greek *ekklesia*. Both mean "to call out." There has long been too much emphasis on churches as physical structures. I have been a daily Mass-goer for years, and I too have associated the Mass with a building. But this crisis has helped me to see that church isn't merely a place. It's a state of mind that calls us out of ourselves to recognize that we are part of something more vast, more mysterious, and more significant. The Quakers probably had the right idea when they called their places of worship "meeting houses." They seem to have recognized a long time ago that the earth is our church. The people around us are the church.

My concept of sacrament is also evolving. As Catholics, we tend to think of sacraments as specific rituals mediated by ordained clergy. If, as we also believe, sacraments are rituals meant to reflect God's grace in the world in a tangible way, then now is the time for us to broaden our thinking. Now is the time to become sacraments for each other—visible, human signs of God's grace in the world.

There won't be the usual packed churches this Easter, with children parading in new outfits, egg hunts, and large family gatherings. A certain stillness will mark this year's celebrations. We will "slide our way past trouble," to paraphrase a line from William Stafford's poem, "Cutting Loose." In his poem "Keeping Quiet," Pablo Neruda speaks of a "huge silence" that can help us to better understand ourselves, as in those times when so much on earth seems dead "and later proves to be alive." We must try to learn from that silence.

Looking beyond the present
to what later proves alive,
Judith

Dear Judith,

It is a cool, quiet morning. A lawn mower hums in the distance. Here at the abbey, no workers come and go. Growing leaves are enhancing the skeletal trees with a softer definition and, for the time being, the trees appear lacelike. The woods are an array of countless shades of color: yellow-green, lemon-green, deep-green, rust, tan, and others that are hard to name. The distant hills appear to wear a sheep-like coat of wool. Later, this varied color and texture will flatten out to a uniform Sherwood green, making the trees barely distinguishable.

Our Holy Week and Easter celebrations were simple and quiet. On Holy Thursday, we waived the traditional washing of the feet as a health precaution, so the service was shorter. I was impressed with the way our abbot introduced the service, enjoining us to "forego much of the solemnity, in order to be in solidarity with the faithful stranded at home" and reminding us that the Church is always greater than its customs and ceremonies and that nothing can keep us from the love of God. He encouraged us to welcome as best we can "this *doing less* and to attune our hearts and minds to how the *Lord* is joining us in our prayers during these days."

As a part of this "doing less," we forewent kissing the wooden cross on Good Friday, instead just bowing reverently. At the Easter Vigil, we did not crowd around the Pascal Fire outside, but stayed in the church, turned toward the exit door, and watched the fire come to life out on the porch. The Pascal candle was blessed, lit, and brought down an aisle near the monks' stalls. There were no Easter lilies to be seen, but fortunately, our redbuds and pink dogwoods were both in full bloom and served to grace the sanctuary.

In Church documents, the monks' community prayer offered during the Liturgy of the Hours and at Mass are called "the prayers of the Church." At this time of crisis, this is true in a special way, as these are the only prayers offered up in a communal form. Of course, other prayers are being said in other churches, but it is only in monasteries and religious houses that prayers are prayed by many gathered together in one body. This thought is striking. But our prayers this Easter seemed no different; all seemed as usual. And perhaps that is as it should be. The prayer of the whole Church is something ordinary and usual. But in this current poverty is the poverty of

Christ, who chose to dwell among us as ordinary and undistinguished.

Some may complain that they cannot pray as effectively at home as they can in church. Others may say that they can pray *more* effectively at home than in church. I have to say that I often cannot pray very effectively either in my room or in church. But that is the way of prayer for a monk who is getting on in years. The fact that I can do either and both *at all* is reason for gratitude, and gratitude is the real core of prayer. Would that I could be more mindful of this from day to day.

Thanks for your sharing and letting your hair down. Keep your chin up. I'll keep my beard up, but can't let down what stubby hair is left on my shaven head.

Yours in Easter joy at this extraordinary time,
Br. Paul

USELESS CARE

Dear Brother Paul,

Hard to believe it is once again June. Half a year gone already. It is as if, once we reached April, the days slid down a steep slope. The big excitement of my day so far was spotting a fox in our front yard. Not something you'd expect to see on a lawn in a college town. It's amazing how proportional these animals are, their elongated heads nicely symmetrical to the rest of their bodies. It didn't get into any mischief, merely sniffed at some petunias in a flower box at the end of our front walkway. I tried to snap a photo of it, but the light was wrong and it wandered off as quickly as it arrived.

Just a few days ago, I had pulled Antoine de St. Exupery's *The Little Prince* from a bookshelf and reread the chapter that tells of the prince's encounter with a fox who schools him on friendship and love. The prince is in love with a rose, but not quite sure what draws him to it. The fox explains that this rose is unique in all the field because the prince has cared for it, watered it, and built a screen around it to protect it from caterpillars. To paraphrase Mary Oliver, we care for the things we love, but we also learn to love the things we care for.

Since I last wrote you, I have been to two more meditation sessions with Lama Tsering. I promised myself that I would meditate daily. Alas, my good intentions seem to have evaporated like this morning's mist. Perhaps that isn't exactly true. You could say some fragile plumes remain in the form of micro-meditations, little pauses I take throughout the day—like the coffee breaks we take at the office. The best meditation time for me seems to be right after I wake up, especially on days when I rise before dawn. I lie there listening to the birds, trying to empty my mind and rest in the moment. I'm always glad when I take the time for these pauses. They aren't merely an excuse not to get on to some "more important" task.

Cooking is actually another of my meditative practices. It becomes an occasion for self-abandonment. Maybe it's the repetitive action of cutting vegetables, slicing fruit, or sautéing potatoes that puts me in a mindless state. I often escape to the kitchen when I hit a rough patch in a piece of writing. It gives my mind just enough time to lie fallow and let some fertile ideas break through. I trust that, as a cook yourself, you've experienced something similar.

Still, the candy store of distractions beckons. Even when I am not meditating, my attention gets drawn toward a scattershot of matters that have nothing to do with what I *should* be doing or want to accomplish. When someone asks me to do something, I'm like an alcoholic who can't pass up a drink. I tend to say "yes" to just about every request, whether it's to write an endorsement for a new book, or serve on a board, or write an article for a publication, or give a talk—just fill in the blank. Distraction upon distraction. I wonder if you experience some of the same, or if the built-in structures of your Trappist life shield you from too many scattered activities.

Sometimes I feel like the Zen monk Tetsugen, whose goal was to have the Buddha's sutras printed in Japanese from 7,000 woodblocks. After years of criss-crossing Japan seeking donations, he finally collected enough funds. Then the river Uji overflowed and thousands were left homeless. Tetsugen used the money he had collected to help the homeless and immediately began raising a second round of funds for the woodblocks. Just when he had managed to collect the amount he needed, an epidemic spread across the country. (Sound familiar?) Tetsugen donated the money he had collected to help the sick and set out a third time to raise the funds for the woodblocks. Twenty years later, he finally fulfilled his original dream of printing the sutras in Japanese. Decades had passed in the meantime!

Tetsugen's story does have a happy ending, however. The printing blocks used to create that first Japanese edition of the Buddhist texts still exist. They are on display at a monastery in Kyoto. The Japanese tell their children that Tetsugen is actually responsible for three editions of the sutras, and that the first two—caring for the homeless and caring for the sick—are far superior to the final, printed edition. When I think of Tetsugen, I sometimes fear that I will not have enough time to complete all of my projects. But then an inner voice tells me not to worry so much about what I do or don't accomplish. Just let go. Let what will be, be.

At our last meditation session, someone asked Lama Tsering what he finds most difficult about his work as a hospital chaplain. He said that, just when he thinks he may be making a difference in someone's life, the patient is released from the hospital or dies. When asked how he deals with that, he answered: "Non-attachment." By not being so attached to a particular outcome, he could see the value in simply accepting what is. This reminded me of what I have been reading in Merton's essay "A Life Free from Care," in which he warns about creating for ourselves "little worlds" of anxiety and useless care.

In terms of letting go of distractions, I may be making some progress. At a time when I was trying to decide whether to accept an invitation to serve as president of yet another volunteer organization, a friend sent me a passage from *Essentialism: The Disciplined Pursuit of Less* by Greg McKeown. A "non-essentialist," according to McKeown, says "yes" to requests without much reflection, feeling obligated to do so because the request seems "all important." This inevitably leads to issues about "how to fit it all in." An "essentialist," on the other hand, reflects on what really matters and says: "I choose to." I think that I have been a non-essentialist for too long. And yet, I hope the detours I have made may still prove valuable in their own right, the way Tetsugen's detours proved meaningful. Perhaps I will still manage, despite deviations along the way, to reach my goals—just as he did.

Yours in the detours,
Judith

Dear Brother Paul,

Just finished reading Merton's final address as novice director to the Gethsemani monks before he went off to live as a hermit. I loved it! I had to write you right away, because Merton's words are so in line with what we have been discussing about non-attachment.

Merton tells the monks: "There is one basic, essential thing in the monastic life and in the Christian life, the thing that we all seek in one way or another. It is some assurance that it is possible in this kind of life *"to put away all care."* This doesn't mean walking around with a dismissive attitude toward everything, however. Rather it's about dispensing with *useless care*—the kind of care that arises because we "cannot confront the inevitable fact of death." We travel, Merton says, in circular lines in an effort to forget that we are all on a straight path to the grave. For him, choosing the life of a hermit was, in a way, like choosing a kind of death—death to society, death to certain creature comforts, consolations, and support. He describes it as casting aside our fear of death by placing all our fears in the hands of God.

This is the opposite of creating "little worlds of care" for ourselves, Merton says. He finds a kindred spirit in the French Jesuit Jean Pierre de Caussade, who, in *Abandonment to Divine Providence,* writes: "Since God offers to take . . . care of our affairs, let us once and for all abandon them to [God's] infinite wisdom." This is fundamentally what love is, Merton says. When you love another person, you forget yourself. "This is what God asks of us," he explains, "to live in such a way that we don't have to think about ourselves. [God] will think about us . . . so you are no longer worrying about whether you are virtuous or not, you just live. You live without care and without concern for anything of yourself."

I wonder if what I have been labeling as distraction and lack of attentiveness to my work is actually a halting, unconscious attempt to live without care. If had to choose something that I did in the past twenty-four hours that was essential, I would say it was the four hours I spent weeding in our garden. I came back into the house drenched in sweat. It was exhilarating.

Merton provides a fascinating image for the world of care. He compares it to an opaque package. When we rid ourselves of useless care, the world begins to look less like a package covered in layers of wrapping, and more like a transparent bowl. Life becomes more transparent. People become more transparent. Even the rabbits he encounters in the fields become transparent. And God is in all, he says. "The rabbitness of God is shining through all those darn rabbits."

This is "the great joy that the Lord is present and living in this world," Merton concludes. "*Dominus vobiscum.*" The Lord with us. Perhaps in some unconscious way, by not focusing so much on what I think I need to *do,* I am trying to forget about myself. Perhaps I am trying to leave a larger space for God to work in my life, instead of constantly reaching for the controls.

Yours in the rabbitness of rabbits,
Judith

Dear Judith,

Let me begin with the goal of non-attachment. That is pretty much the whole issue, isn't it? It pertains not only to the projects and goals we set for ourselves in this life, but also to the spiritual life itself. We must have goals and take means to an end, but the results are in the hands of God in the long run.

We complicate the spiritual life with our impure motives. Ambition creeps in and sets up spirituality as an achievement to be won—something with clear ends and satisfying results. The process is far more paradoxical than that, however. Real spiritual satisfaction is not what it is imagined to be. As Saint John of the Cross says: "To reach satisfaction in all, desire its possession in nothing."

I have a desire to live the monastic life, but I also have an ambition to have a foot in the intellectual world. These can be conflicting desires. One recent dream took me back to the time when I was studying in Chicago. In the dream, I was trying to get to class on time but I could not find the room, or even the school. In another recurring dream, I was expected to make a presentation and people were waiting, but I was late. In yet another,

I kept missing classes. In other dreams, my ambition to live the monastic life encountered frustrating obstacles. In one of these, I had finished a course and needed to get back to the monastery in time for Vespers, but I got lost in the middle of the city and couldn't find my way to the Interstate that would lead me home. In my personal dream language, the complexities of a city often seem to represent the intellectual life and the obstacles I encounter pursuing it.

If I were perfectly free of attachment, I would no longer care about how well I am living both the monastic life and the intellectual life. I would be engaged in both while possessing neither. And that is the lesson we must learn—to be both engaged and free. This is a task that needs to be taken up every day anew. I have not given up thinking I may make progress in that sense. But as John of the Cross says: "To come to be what you are not, you must go by a way in which you are not." Within that "unknown way," how do you distinguish between what is essential and what is nonessential? To what must I say "no" and to what do I say "yes?" Is the way wide open and free? Or is it the narrow way?

Perhaps there is a lesson to be found in the rabbits I encounter. This spring, I regularly pass four or five of them while walking to my meditation spot. They seem to be unafraid of me, at ease with my passing, and unconcerned with what they will do next. But there is another rabbit that I encounter elsewhere that immediately runs for its life when it sees me in the evening. It too knows what is essential, or thinks it does, for I have no ill intention on its life. What these rabbits have in common is that they all inhabit specific areas—I always find them in their same respective regions. That is part of the "essential living" they do without knowing it—that, and taking a nibble of grass when they feel like it. Neither the rabbits who stay around me nor the rabbit who runs away are either correct or incorrect. They are what they are.

I remember well the words Father Louis spoke to us before he left to take up the hermit's life. Like you, I was struck by his comment that we view life as an opaque package with something inside. We take off the wrapping only to find another layer. We keep taking off layers of wrapping and come to find, in the end, that there is *nothing* there. His point isn't that life is an empty void, but rather that everything is obvious. The sacredness of everything is obvious and we are missing it. God is evident all around, even in the rabbits. In the rabbits, we see "the rabbitiness of God." As quirky a phrase as any of his.

In the Eastern rite of our Church, there is a ritual for the installation of a hermit. The monks go out in procession to the mountain where the hermit will live and leave him to a life free of care where he can be "kissed by God." An endearing phrase. You have been given your yard of grass to cultivate in life, just as I have been given mine. The real challenge is to be unattached to preconceived notions of what the outcome of our actions should be, to be at rest with that which is, to be "kissed by God."

Yours free of useless care (at least in this moment),
Br. Paul

NATURE'S MAGIC SPOTS

Dear Judith,

This summer, I have taken to spending thirty to forty minutes in silence after Mass, letting the mystery soak in and becoming more sensitive to the beauty of the morning and more grateful for the life I live. One morning about a month ago, I took a slow meditative walk to a place about twelve minutes from the monastery. I will share with you the words I wrote about that morning:

> With the sun already risen and patches of fog in
> the valley, I wrap in a green cloak against the chill
> and walk past the shop buildings, past the garage,
> past the sandstone wall where swallows circle
> like high skaters on air, smoothly curving, clean
> as lines of Gregorian chant. I pass the places
> where rabbits daily run across my path, taking a
> few hops as I near. I go eastward on the straight
> dirt road, under the row of oak trees, toward the
> external enclosure wall with fields on both sides
> streaked by sunlight. One tree hides the sun—a

*burning tree that is not consumed—where God
speaks the word "be."*

*Today I will not stop and sit on the bench
against the wall facing the sun that filters through
the forest. I will go all the way to the darkened
end where the path dips into what we call St.
Anne's park. There, on either side, two boxwood
shrubs have grown to full stature to form a gate-
way. The ground inside is thick with dark-green
vinca vine. It is a fairy place full of secrets, where
rare wood thrushes exchange liquid chimes,
where a common dove answers a distant friend
deeper in the woods. Tiny twit-twit birds briefly
stay and quickly go. On the floor under this vault
stand weeds, leaves spreading, all of one kind,
short and graceful. These, you know, are fairies
occupying a ball room, spaced out, some large,
some small.*

*I come across an old bench, but do not sit
there. I settle instead on the stone-built pedes-
tal where the statue of St. Benedict once stood,
facing the enclosure wall that borders the quiet
court, which is handsome with sunlight and tree
shadow. Each individual plant I see is of a mind
to be there, just where it is, where the world does
not see it—each a young, light green; each a faint
breath of magic; each adding to this leafy hall
that hides magic of several kinds.*

*Alone here a while, I silently learn that noth-
ing is alone. Here is a courtyard full of beings.*

Here I can stay only briefly. Here I can only wait
until sunlight streaks the floor and grows from
gold to white. I do not know the language here;
my ears are too dense to hear. It is only courtesy
for me to leave.

Such were my impressions of the hour. And you, Judith?
Do you ever find such fortunate times and places? I
hope so.

Reflectively yours,
Br. Paul

Dear Brother Paul,

You draw a wonderful mental picture for me of your
meditation walks. I feel as though I am walking along
with you—just as, when reading Merton's famous essay
"Fire Watch," I feel that I am strolling with him in his
rubber-soled shoes as he saunters through the abbey's
shadowy corridors and climbs up creaking stairways
into its sweltering, cramped rafters as dusk descends. I
remember our many often-wordless hikes together across
the monastery's hay fields, past cypresses growing tall and
full, stopping here and there to admire a mayapple in the
underbrush, or chew on a sassafras leaf. What a marvel-
ous prelude such walks must be to your quiet meditation.

I would say my own meditation efforts are improv-
ing, although they are not nearly as deep or exhilarating
as yours. I am learning a great deal from Lama Tsering,
with whom I meet once a month online. He spent our last

two sessions speaking about the lotus mantra for purity of heart: *om mani padme hum*. When I wake, I spend some time seated on the edge of the bed, my feet flat on the floor, hands joined together under my chin, and quietly repeat the mantra dozens of times.

Lama Tsering says that, before he prays, he calls to mind all of his past teachers, both living and deceased. He tries to feel the breath of each of them flowing through him, going back even to the Buddha. That touched me deeply. Before I meditate, I now try to call to mind my many teachers: the Sister who taught me to love myth, medieval art, and baroque music; the Jesuit priests I encountered in college who encouraged me to be "a person for others"; the Benedictine sisters who continue to school me in compassion. And you, Brother Paul, who showed me how to appreciate small moments of beauty and think in nonlinear ways.

I struggle a great deal with mental distractions, but less so when I recite the lotus mantra. I often had trouble with centering prayer, breathing mindfully and silently repeating the same "sacred" word. By contrast, I like hearing myself whisper *om mani padme hum*. I love the way the words feel as they emerge from my lips. I take in a deep breath and, as I let it out, I utter the six syllables. This keeps my mind on both my prayer and my breathing.

In our most recent session, Lama Tsering spoke of the power of breath as it relates to the corona virus. We can contract the deadly virus by breathing it in, and we can infect others by breathing it out. Can we not then use our breath to spread loving kindness by breathing in compassion and breathing out peace? Praying the lotus mantra sends remedies into the universe for the many emotions that can afflict us. Each word carries a particular meaning. *Om* evokes generosity; *ma*, ethical behavior; *ni*, patience; *pad*, perseverance; *me*, selflessness; *hum*, wisdom. These words are bulwarks against the afflictions of greed, aggression, anger, jealousy, prejudice, impatience, and ignorance.

Another of my meditation "places" these days is our screened-in front porch. This is where I go to think and write, until the humidity gets too oppressive or the mosquitoes become too aggressive. Insects seem to have uncanny ways of letting themselves inside our screens. Nonetheless, the porch is a fine spot to listen for various bird calls. Right now, I hear the tapping of a flicker. Often I hear the staccato whistle of a dickcissel, the *cheer, cheer, cheer* of a cardinal, and, of course, the familiar caws of crows. Sometimes the birdsong combines with the castanet-like snapping of crickets and cicadas.

Our neighborhood is blessed with a wide array of trees, from Chinese elms to black locusts to Japanese maples, and both white and red oaks. My favorite tree is the tall evergreen that stands in the front yard of the house across the street. It reaches about 150 feet high and casts quite a soaring profile against a cloudless blue sky. What is fascinating is that, for a quarter of the way up its trunk, the tree has no branches. Each year it seems to lose a few more, like the hairs of a man going bald. I suppose the tree is slowly dying, yet refuses to give up. Maybe that is why I admire it so much. To look at it gives me courage to persevere.

The late Benedictine writer Macrina Wiederkehr has a lovely passage in her book *Gold in Your Memories*. She writes that everyone should have a "private room," a sort of "magic spot" to which they can retreat, either in person or in their imagination. Hers was a spot in a cornfield near her childhood home. Using a broom she had made out of tall grasses, she "swept an area clean" and spread an old shirt to serve as carpet. "There in that magic spot," she writes, "I would sit for hours and dream."

I think we all need a magic spot, or more than one. And if we don't have one, we would be wise to create one by "sweeping an area clean." That is perhaps what both of us are doing in our meditation places.

Yours in the quiet, the mantra, and the magic,
Judith

Dear Judith,

It is interesting that you should mention Merton's famous essay "Fire Watch." It brought to mind a strange experience I had when making the rounds of the nightly fire watch, which was once one of the regular duties all of the monks in the community shared. I walked the same tunnels and halls and climbed the same stairs that Merton described. I can still remember the smell of bat guano when climbing up into the steeple tower. I knew every step he had taken. Decades later, I was part of a team that traveled to Prades, France, Merton's birthplace. I found myself seated in the one-room schoolhouse where he had attended classes. There, the leader of our team read "Fire Watch." It was like entering an incredible time warp! There I was, listening to a Mennonite woman from a college in British Columbia, speaking at Merton's school in France about an experience I'd lived through many times at Gethsemani. That a memory so ordinary and particular could be found so far from home moved me deeply. It was as if it had escaped from time and space and landed before me in this stone building in the shadow of the Pyrenees. I loved it.

You never know what insignificant details in life may reach beyond yourself—like the mustard seed that eventually grows into a tree and spreads out its branches. Life, when lived in prayer, is never confined to one existence. Who knows where it will go?

I am glad you are focusing on purity of heart with the Lama. That is the principle theme of the Desert Fathers as found in the writings of St. John Cassian—the purity of heart for those who would see God. I have not tried practicing the *om mani padme hum* mantra, but I do start every day going through ninety-nine beads and saying the Jesus prayer: *Lord, Jesus Christ, son of the living God, have mercy on me.* Once I begin, I go on to beg mercy for all, and then for specific individuals—family, friends, and "enemies." I like to do this most of all in the early hours of the morning when the stars are clear and I can lie on my back on my mattress in the yard and face the universe. It is a lot for one monk to pray for, but we each have our mustard seed to add.

I do wrestle with a certain conundrum regarding "purity of heart," however. On the one hand, all the wealth and magic of nature surrounds me. On the other hand, I know that the poor of heart cling only to the God who is unseen—the truly "unknown God." For them, all else is set aside for "the one thing necessary." The anonymous author of *The Cloud of Unknowing* and the Dominican Meister Eckhardt address this point strongly, and I love their writings. However, I have so much of beauty, art, and nature in my life and I continue to avail myself of them, with no real accounting for why I do so. Perhaps no accounting is called for. Life lived in a search for God has done much over the years to relieve me of a need to cling to these things. For that reason, I can turn to them free of attachment and enjoy them purely as a gift; I can take them as they come or leave them as they go. And when they do come in fullness, they eventually leave me with some emptiness. There is something at the center that says: "We are not Him."

To willfully seek emptiness is dangerous. A holy willfulness ends up making you full of nothing but your own will. The real emptiness must come through God. It is a grace given as a poverty that is not even your own. It is a simplicity that comes as a child-like contentment, precisely because it is not your own. I have much yet to feel of this, or maybe much of it is there already but I don't feel it self-consciously. If so, that makes it all the better. Let me be wary of self-congratulations. The measure of all things interior is unseen and yet to come.

Reading Buddhist teachers gives me some appreciation for emptiness. It gives me some vocabulary about it. But in the end, I claim no understanding. It would be a mistake to do so. I am honored that you count me among your "teachers," but it is a mistake to do so. I hardly know from one day to the next where to go, or whether there is anywhere to go.

> Let us remain beginners—and
> remain beginners together,
> Br. Paul

CULTIVATING SILENCE

Dear Judith,

One of the topics I've wanted to write to you about is my love of silence, which is so essential to the contemplative life. It is something that deserves watchfulness and care if you want to have it. Now that our Order has a more flexible practice of silence than in the past, it is up to the individual to secure his own silence. Of course, silence is already built into our daily practice. We observe the "Grand Silence" from 8:00 at night until 8:00 in the morning—those hours when everything is still. This is the time for Vigils, private prayer, and reading. Likewise, there are rooms where we cannot talk and places where we can, and although these restrictions are loosely observed, they are respected enough to be helpful.

When I entered the monastery in the late Fifties, our observance was so strict that you could almost have called it a cult of silence. In the writings of Thomas Merton, however, you find something much deeper than that. He sought a culture of silence that surrounds prayer and contemplation and is derived from it. This interior appreciation seems to be what characterizes silence as it is practiced at the abbey today. We are no longer so preoccupied with silence that we complain about its being broken. Now our silence has a more natural quality.

Underneath this physical silence lies the inner silence we each must cultivate. A silent mind brings about a silent presence. When I was young, anxious, and restless, one of the priests gave me the nickname "Grandslam" because, when working in the kitchen, I was often so concerned to get things done that I was not aware of how much noise I was making around others. I punished my own ears with that noise as well, but I have since learned to be easier on myself. Stress creates noise and noise creates stress, all without our knowing it.

I have always thought that the art of haiku conveys the *experience* of silence. Haiku lets silence speak. It communicates a taste of silence, a feeling of what silence is in our finer moments. It conveys personal experiences without speaking of the experiences as personal.

Here are a few of my own haiku that I hope illustrate what I mean. First, there is the silence to be found in outward things. It is almost irresistible when we see it snowing.

No silence is so
silent as silence of snow.
Only the slow wind knows.

The very interaction of snow and light wind suggests some secret at which we can only guess. But to sit and listen for a while allows it to suggest itself.

Each snowflake descends
with some secret to whisper—
soft intimacies.

This can only happen when you are already present to
yourself, already in the home of intimacy, which is your
silent meditation. In that moment, there is something
more than yourself. You need only wait to let it come.

I wait in silence
while silence waits in me—with
Love in the balance.

"Love in the balance" can mean different things. It could
be that still moment when you weigh out the sugar and the
scale sways and comes to a standstill. It could be a scale
balanced in the outstretched hand of Justice when much is
to be lost or gained. It could be the attribute of love itself,
in which grace comes to balance what was lacking. I like to
think it is the latter. In silence, love comes gracefully and is
a loving grace, the way I imagine angels arriving:

Angels are silver
hinges on gates to meaning
swung on silent bolts.

Saints, too, are hinges on gates to meaning, as are unseen
friends, living and dead, who lead us to the quiet home of
the heart. It is good to be in a place that is so silent you
can hear your own heartbeat.

May many such moments be yours.
May the culture of silence be yours.

Br. Paul

Dear Brother Paul,

Your description of silence in the monastery brings me
back to an experience I had on one of my first extended
visits to Gethsemani. I was in the library having a conversation with my husband and another guest, talking at
a normal volume, when one of the monks passed by. He
put his thumb to his ear and fluttered his other fingers. I
asked you later what that gesture meant. You said it was
part of the sign language the monks once used. It meant
"I can hear you." The monk was essentially telling us
to shut up. He didn't do it as most librarians would. He
didn't *shush* us or whisper to us to be quiet. He told us
to stop talking, but did it silently. Our voices must have
sounded jarring and intrusive within the overall silence of
the monastery.

    I have only encountered what I would call a pure
experience of silence a few times in my life. I wrote
about one of those experiences in my book *Atchison
Blue*. On my first visit to Mount St. Scholastica Monastery in Atchison, I sat alone one morning in the choir
chapel. Silence saturated the room. At one point, I
looked up at the stained-glass window in front of me
and saw St. Benedict standing with outstretched arms.
Surrounding him were some words from *The Rule* in
Latin: *omni tempore silentio debent studere*—"At all
times, cultivate silence." It was as if the paradox I had
been living was staring down at me. I had been running
around the country, talking and talking, trying to help
other people live a more contemplative life, when what

was missing in my own life were moments of silence and solitude when I could simply listen and be. Before that day, I had stood under a vast canvas of stars in the Utah desert, walked the edge of the Yorkshire moors, and gazed down from the heights of Red Rocks Mountain in Colorado—all places of extreme quiet. Yet I had never before experienced such a profound depth of silence as I did that morning in the chapel. It moved me to tears.

I love the postcards in your abbey gift shop that say: "Silence Spoken Here." And I find it interesting that the first thing visitors see upon arriving at the abbey is a 19th-century graveyard. Who are more silent than the dead? A few feet farther along is the path leading to the abbey church, where a sign says: "Silence." Just beyond that is the gate that says: "God Alone."

Whenever I visit the abbey, I have the sense of entering a deeper reality, one where my soul—and not my head, for a change—is leading my steps. Monasteries and Quaker meeting houses may be among the last places on earth to practice what St. Benedict calls "esteem for silence." I read recently that decibel levels have increased even in such remote places as Alaska's Denali National Park. No nature preserve can be truly silent. There is the sound of wind, and birds, and passing vehicles. I've visited the Egyptian desert, where early monks and monastic women went to escape the clamor and temptations of cities. Happily there are still vast stretches of quiet, uninhabited areas in that desert—if you get far enough away from the souvenir hawkers and the tourists lining up to enter the pyramids or ride on an elephant.

Some of the worst intrusions we experience today come, not from sounds we hear, but from the "white noise" of texts, email, and social media. My email inbox dings constantly with announcements for some new webinar or workshop, a retreat or conference, or an online lecture. Every once in a while, I need to take a break from all of the messaging or I fear I will go crazy. Of course, when I stay away from email or social media for a few days, my inbox fills with messages from people asking me if I'm all right, because they haven't heard from me lately!

I often chuckle when you tell me that you are preparing for yet another interview on yet another podcast. Apparently our 24/7 system of connecting has infiltrated even such bastions of silence as Trappist abbeys. Merton made this wise observation about technology:

> The whole massive complex of technology,
> which reaches into every aspect of social life
> today, implies a huge organization of which no
> one is really in control, and which dictates its
> own solutions irrespective of human needs or
> even of reason. Technology now has reasons
> entirely its own which do not necessarily take
> into account the needs of man.

It's not that the technology we use to communicate is inherently bad. It's that we must face the danger of drowning in its rapid currents.

Like you, I believe that silence isn't something we seek only in a physical setting. It is a habit of the heart, an interior peace we cultivate. That is likely what Abba Moses, one of the early monks of the Egyptian desert, meant when he told a young monk seeking "a word" about the contemplative life: "Sit in your cell and your cell will teach you everything."

Answers often come to me when I am doing nothing in particular, just sitting in silence. This is the way that Elijah heard the still, small voice of God. When it is not possible to escape the bustle and noise around me, I often retreat to a place in my mind. I imagine that I am sitting on a wood block under the fig tree that my Italian grand-father planted in the backyard of my parents' home. This is where I went as a child to think and dream and write poems. Even in the middle of a crowded, noisy room, I can go to that mental place and feel myself almost liter-ally floating above the chaos around me.

I had a similar experience once with you. Before dawn one morning, the two of us stepped out in silence onto the portico of the abbey church after Vigil prayers had ended. As we stood gazing up at Venus and the Milky Way, I felt something of what the psalmist must have experienced when he wrote:

> When I consider your heavens,
> the work of your fingers,
> the moon and the stars
> which you have set in place,
> what is mankind that you are mindful of them,
> human beings that you care for them?

My favorite part of the day is the time just before dawn when the neighbors' houses are quiet and dark and the streets are empty. As Merton once observed: "The most wonderful moment of the day is when creation asks permission to be." I step out on our front lawn. There are just the flickering stars, the waking birds, the thrumming insects, and me. Not really silence, but sounds that feed my interior silence. I can at least feel, if not really hear, my own heartbeat.

Yours in the quiet home of the heart,
Judith

LIVING IN ETERNITY

Dear Judith,

It occurred to me that death and resurrection have come up several times in our letters while trying to answer the question of what constitutes a life of meaning. I have developed some ideas of my own from a philosophical point of view that I would like to share. My thinking starts with the idea of eternity and spins outward from there.

St. Augustine defines eternity as *toto simul,* all things together as one. Thus, eternity is not to be considered as contradictory to time, but includes all time, and all space as well. Everything is included in the eternal *now.* Our experience of time is discreet, one moment after another; but in eternity, time is one "now." That is because God is pure simplicity and the consciousness of God includes all things in that simplicity. God has an eternal consciousness of what is, what was, and what is to come.

When we die, our minds are released from the individuated condition caused by being anchored in matter. We have a new freedom in awareness and, as we draw closer to God, we draw closer to that eternal consciousness. I doubt that this happens all at once. Or maybe it does in some sense. But the point is that what we ultimately find in God is all things *as God is aware of them*, timelessly and from all eternity. Time is embraced in eternity.

God is eternally aware even of this body that I somehow now am, as well as all the history I have lived. From this point of view, the resurrected body is the one I already inhabit, but seen from God's perspective. This body can touch and be touched, but it can still be seen from God's eternal point of view. All that it is and all that has been is illuminated by eternity, just more vivid and more real when seen from the perspective of the whole.

Everything I am and do in the present remains in eternity, but it does not remain static, like an old photograph or an instant replay of a sports event. I like to think that the body evolves to a new level, just as an acorn grows into an oak tree. The tree has the same *being* as the acorn, but is so changed that you cannot recognize it. St. Paul speaks in similar terms about the grain of wheat that is sown and produces a whole stalk of wheat, complete with a new head of grain.

The resurrection of the body will be a great transformation. I like to think of it as a fractal—a complex never-ending pattern. If you start with one fractal of one unique shape, it can replicate itself into a gorgeous shape that looks nothing like the original fractal. Consequently, what evolves in the resurrection is determined by the shape we have taken for ourselves in this life, for good or for ill. The outcome has the same reality as the original shape, but transformed. I like St. Gregory of Nyssa's idea that our eternity will be an unlimited process of moving toward God. God is infinite and there is no end to our journey toward him. The resurrected body is integral to the process of getting there.

The same may be happening, not only with our bodily shape, but also with our time as we live it. Perhaps not only our bodies, but our history is taken up in resurrection. Each day is eternally present in the consciousness of God. We pass through; we leave it behind; it fades. But God's mind never fades. And in the resurrection of our bodies, we become more aware of every act and happening seen as part of the totality—seen from God's point of view. That must be what we mean by the Last Judgment. In this view, we make the judgment as well, as it becomes clear what each act, each feeling, each thought, each desire actually *is*.

I like to think that each day is like a new DNA element laid out in a gene. Each day, we form the organism that we will become. But what we see now is immeasurably different from what the developed organism becomes. That developed organism is the resurrected body, yet it is the same organism contained in the DNA from which it developed.

We blindly assume that we know what the body is. Although we puzzle over the resurrection of the body, we never really question what the body is. The body is something we experience every day, so we take for granted that we really know it. But physics has proved that cells and molecules and atoms are mostly empty space. Not only that, our bodies renew all their cells every seven years.

So which of these assemblages of cells is resurrected? But let's assume that we do *not* know the body. Through his death and Resurrection, Christ teaches us what our whole humanity is, and he continues teaching beyond this stage of existence. We have yet to find out what the body really is.

Consequently, I am hesitant to accept what is described in pious literature about heaven. We really don't *know* what it will be like. We can only be open-minded and have faith in what is beyond our present apprehension. We are just at the beginning of it all—babes still in the womb, who are far from knowing what they really are.

This is all speculation on my part, of course. Just things I like to think about. These and other notions about the resurrected body are only given us in clues and hints. How is it that Jesus and Mary can hear every prayer from every part of the world, many rising at the same time? Not exactly something within the capacity of a single human body as we know it. I suspect that there is much to be learned from our devotional and sacramental practices that may illuminate the mystery of the Resurrection.

What does this say about personal relationships? I know you and you know me. But wait. I hardly know myself—at least not, as yet, in the totality of what I will be. The little letters we write, the casual contacts we make in life, the fragments of acquaintance, the relationships broken or made whole are just the beginning. Each is a small seed of what can develop in eternity. None of it is ever lost. Nothing is ever lost.

Yours in eternity,
Br. Paul

Dear Brother Paul,

Your meditation on eternity fills me with wonder, but also solace and hope. I am going to need to rest with your words for a long while. They are deeper than anything I have come across in my all-too-shallow understanding of the spiritual life. You give me much to think about.

Funny that you should write about this now. Thoughts of eternity have emerged for me as well in recent weeks, although in a totally different context. In one of your letters several months ago, you mention the writings of the 12th-century English monk St. Aelred of Rievaulx. I had been meaning for a long time to delve into his famous work, *Spiritual Friendship,* but had the chance to do so only lately. I was impressed by Aelred's declaration that true friendship is *eternal*. It is part of the ongoing order of creation and one of the ways we experience intimations of eternity in this life. That is how I feel about our exchanges—that through them I have somehow been experiencing a small taste of eternity.

I'd like to think that you and I fit St. Aelred's definition of true friends as two hearts speaking to one another. In these letters, we have entrusted to one another, as he would say, "the contents of our heart." What makes true friendship is that our hearts are not drawn to one another by hope of gain, but by mutual goodwill.

By Aelred's definition, friends of the heart need not be afraid to correct one another. Their motive stems always from what he calls *benevolentia*—goodwill—and *caritas*—charity and love. The model here is Christ. Human friendship makes us a friend of God, and that friendship, he says, is a step toward "the knowledge of God." A true friend, a spiritual friend, becomes "a guardian of love," and more, a "guardian of [our] soul."

A friendship that ceases to exist was not true friendship to begin with, Aelred says, for a true friend "loves always." Reflecting on that thought, I take heart that my bond with my friend A. will endure. Yes, our interests, habits, work, and family lives have diverged over the years. Still, I think I can speak for both of us when I say that we will continue to share the true measure of friendship. We will "love always."

You and I will likewise "love always." I recently picked up an old issue of *Parabola* and found an essay of yours adapted from your memoir, *In Praise of the Useless Life*. You wrote it after a spending a week on retreat at the Merton hermitage. You share that you "came to the hermitage in need of cutting free again." Your first evening there, you put a scherzo by Bruckner on the CD player and stepped outside to look up at the half moon. Soon, you were swaying to the music in a half circle. You tossed your white shirt in the air "as if it were a cloud," and started to dance, "lifting and pulling, tossing and dropping, working hands, stretching arms." Dancing with abandon. Then it hit me: This is it. This is what you have been trying to tell me all along. This is *how to be*.

Perhaps the anxiety and restlessness I often experience doesn't stem from a dearth of achievements, but from a paucity of "cutting free." That is the struggle that so many of us over-achievers face. Today, I slept most of the day. Now I am feeling wide awake again. I've begun writing a new poem. Maybe, in this instance, sleep was my way of dancing.

Next time we see each other, let's dance—I mean really, actually, physically dance. Outside Merton's hermitage, preferably. Barefoot if possible. I will bring an extra shirt to toss into the air with you.

Yours in anticipation,
Judith

ACKNOWLEDGMENTS

The authors wish to extend our gratitude to Greg Brandenburgh of Hampton Roads Publishers, who gave generously of his time to shepherd this book, Jane Hagaman and Laurie Trufant for their artful editing, our agent Amanda Annis of Trident Media Group for believing in this project from the start, Abbot Elias Dietz and the monks of the Abbey of Gethsemani for their prayers and moral support, and the spirit of Thomas Merton, who continues to inspire us endlessly.

HOW TO BE

Study Guide

INTRODUCTION:
SEEDS OF A FRIENDSHIP

Judith Valente writes that "letters are the remnants we leave to mark important episodes in our lives ... We introduce ourselves, confide our hopes, confess our errors, offer our thanks, and say goodbye in letters."

Welcome to the study guide for *How to Be*. This study guide is your opportunity to join the conversation between Judith Valente and Brother Paul. You can use this guide in different ways. If you belong to a book group or you're studying the book as part of a study group or retreat, the questions can be discussed among members. If you're reading the book on your own, you can answer these questions in a journal—or, after reading each section of the book, you can sit quietly and think about your answers to that section's prompts in a kind of active meditation. However you choose to use this study guide, feel welcome to confide your hopes, confess errors, and offer thanks as you interact with the authors of *How to Be.*

Letter Writing

Valente writes Brother Paul that she is struggling to know when it's time to leave a job. She asks him, "... how do I make that leap when all that's on the other side is uncertainty?" And Brother Paul describes wanting to leave his job cooking in the monastery kitchen, which he used to love—"The music went out of the job."

Detail a time in your life when you knew it was time to change direction, like leaving a job. Be sure to describe how you knew it was time to make that change, as well as your fears about making that change.

"Hope," Valente writes, "allows us to step into the unknown without feeling that we are leaping off a ledge, but rather that we are *learning to walk on air.* That is what I seek. To walk on air."

Now describe how you learned to "walk on air" as you changed direction in your life. Be sure to write about your hopes for the change you were to make, as well as tell about the people in your life who helped you learn "to walk on air."

Being and Doing

Brother Paul writes that he has seen a lot of change at Gethsemani monastery since he entered in 1958—"If you live in a monastery and are unwilling to change, you will become dissatisfied, fixated, and isolated from the rest of the community."

Describe how you manage change in your life. Be sure to tell about the "tools" you use to manage change—like prayer and/or meditation, various communities in which you participate (including family), online resources that help guide you, any "experts" you may consult, etc.

Brother Paul asks Valente a vital question as she considers leaving her job—"Will [leaving] get you closer to God?"

Identify a time in your life when you made a big change, and describe how that change brought "you closer to God."

After Valente resigns from her job, she finds she has time for a lot of different activities. "There are days," she writes, "when I feel totally inefficient, 'useless' to use your word. It's somewhat refreshing."

Describe any days in which you may have experienced being "useless" and/or "inefficient." Be sure to tell how that uselessness/inefficiency made you feel and/or changed how you see yourself. Finally, identify any current opportunities you may have to pursue "uselessness."

Resurrection and Poetry

Brother Paul writes that ". . . the best things in life cost everything. . . . Yesterday brought me a free gift: a long gentle rain."

Describe what you think Brother Paul means by "the best things in life cost everything." Explain how "the free gift of rain" may come with a cost and identify that cost. Be sure to tell of a time when you experienced a "free gift" during an ordinary day and tell what it may have cost you to experience it.

Valente poses two questions based on the poetry of Mary Oliver: "What is the gift we should bring to the world? What is the life that we should live?"

Share your answers to these questions. Be sure to tell about your own life experiences in your answers.

Brother Paul encourages Valente to "waste time"— "Some think that we waste our time walking along the ocean, gazing at wild geese in the sky. Indeed, a good way of getting over the feeling that you are wasting your time is to go out and waste more of it. Waste it intentionally . . . get away from the feeling that the world will crumble without you."

Describe the last time you wasted time, and be as detailed as possible—how did wasting that time make you feel? What did you learn about yourself by wasting time? How do you plan to waste more time in the future?

"I've always loved," writes Valente, "how St. Benedict, in his Rule for monastics, stresses listening. In essence, listening is a kind of waiting—a suspension of activity in favor of being."

Describe how you incorporate (or would like to incorporate) this kind of listening into your life. Be sure to tell what you hear (or would like to hear) by "listening."

Brother Paul describes how he thinks of heaven, as "simply this present world seen from the perspective of eternity and contained in eternity—the mind more vivid and powerful than anything we experience of mind now, or for that matter, of love."

Describe how you imagine heaven. Feel free to build on Brother Paul's thoughts or offer a completely different understanding.

LIVING AND DYING

Brother Paul writes, "The advantage of celebrating a death with the gathering of family and friends is that you get an overview of life lived. The life becomes apparent as a whole. . . . It dawned on me that these people [who had died] are more themselves now than they ever were. They have stepped away from the drowsiness of the dying process and walked into a clear consciousness."

Think of someone you love who has died. Describe their life as a whole, from your perspective. Be as detailed as you can. You may want to think about these questions to get you started: How did they live? How did they die? And who were they, really, in life? How do you see their total personality/life force now that they are gone? What effects did their life have on you, others, and the world?

"The whole of life," Brother Paul writes, "is a dying process, and we waste much of it being something other than what we really are. It is a wandering into the need for this, or away from a fear of that. It is an impersonation of whatever roles the moment demands. Rarely do we settle in to *be*."

Describe who and how you want to *be* at this point in your life. Try to avoid describing yourself in a role or job—instead describe how you want to be as a person, and how you want to be remembered by family and friends.

Brother Paul describes praying the Psalter whenever a monk dies in the monastery. He writes, "In the process of [praying the Psalter], a change occurs. The refutations interiorize the relationship I have with the brother. I go from praying *for* him to praying *with* him. . . . A closeness and immediacy is established and is greater than may have been possible when the monk was alive."

Describe a time when you may have experienced "a closeness and immediacy" with someone who has died. Use as much detail as you can, including any rituals or communities you may have participated in that helped establish that closeness.

Time

"Usually, I am aware of only one particular sliver of time," writes Brother Paul. "One 'now' after another 'now'. . . ." Within the real, there is what leads to the more real, and of that there is no measure. I am most aware of this in meditation, where being present to the moment is most important."

Meditation is a very popular practice. If you meditate, describe how you experience the present or the "now" in meditation. Be sure to describe what you do, as well as your actual experience. If you don't currently meditate, tell why you don't.

Judith Valente writes, ". . . I grew fatigued working at my computer. Instead of forging ahead, battling the tiredness as I usually do, I lay down on the couch and closed my eyes, expecting to take a short nap. I woke up three hours later. . . . I had the sense when I awakened that time had slowed, and I hadn't missed anything at all by not pressing on with work." Rest is a powerful "tool" we can use to experience "being" versus "doing."

Tell how you build (or would like to build) rest into your life as a spiritual, as well as a physical practice. Remember to be detailed—there are a lot of different ways we can "rest," so don't confine yourself to taking naps; describe the effects of rest, not only on yourself, but others; describe how rest affects your spirit; tell how you (or how you would like to) protect/carve out the time to rest.

"... I get caught up in conventional measures of time," writes Valente. "... I find myself grieving over what I didn't accomplish in the last several decades and lamenting that I may not have 'time enough' to do what I'd like to do in the time that remains." Describe your relationship with "time."

Tell how you get "caught up in conventional measures of time." Describe how conventional "clock" time works for you and when it holds you back. If you've ever had an experience of feeling "out of time," or when time was suspended, describe that in detail. Detail any practices or rituals you may use (or would like to use) to step out of time for a while. Also, tell how those practices affect your "being."

Purpose and Call

Judith Valente writes, "I don't think I can be satisfied if the purpose of my life is simply to *be*. I like to take action, to be the heroine of whatever story I am in."

Describe your reaction to Valente's comment—if you agree or disagree, tell why. Describe any time when you may have been skeptical of any encouragement to just "be." Describe why you think/experience the ability to take action is so powerful, and tell why you are, or are not, okay with that.

"A vocation," writes Brother Paul, "is beyond what you might call a purpose in life. I did not find that purpose; my purpose found me. I basically live with a sense of call—and beyond that, a sense of someone calling. . . . It is, I hope, obedience to a freedom that is both mine and greater than mine."

Earlier in the book Valente and Brother Paul write about the importance of being "useless" for those who long to *be*. You were also asked in this study guide to describe your experience of "uselessness." Now, tell how being "useless" fits in (or not) with Brother Paul's understanding of "purpose" and "vocation," and connect that to your own life experience. What is the connection(s) between "useless"-ness and purpose and vocation? How do those connections make sense for people who are not monks or religious professionals? How do you experience (or not) the "freedom" that Brother Paul writes about?

The Hungry Sheep

Valente writes of her feeling "conflicted and sad" with the Church, particularly about its refusal to ordain women to the priesthood. She then declares the reason she stays, despite her sadness: "I often say I remain a Catholic because no one is going to chase me from the Church of my ancestors. I stay, most of all, because I believe in the real presence of Christ in the Eucharist."

Describe a time (and that may be the present time) when you were deeply disappointed by your church. Be sure to tell why you stayed or why you left.

Brother Paul cites a fifty-year-old quote from Thomas Merton: ". . . Today everybody is fighting over who is right. Every side claims to have the answer. . . . People go into agony. It doesn't matter who's right. God is right, hang on to the Lord at the deeper level, and let the others yell." Brother Paul closes with, "Who am I to make an exclusive claim to what is right? God is right."

Whether you stayed or left your church (or moved from one church to another), describe what/who it is that feeds your faith. Tell how you let go (or would like to let go) of claims "to what is right."

Prayer

Brother Paul tells the story of his friend Richard Weingarten, who regularly traveled to many Buddhist sites throughout Asia. "Before leaving for Asia, Richard asked me what I wanted him to bring back for me. I said I did not need anything, but added: 'When you are in a sacred space, in a place of silence, think of me.'"

Describe how you pray, including how you pray for others. Be as detailed as possible. Include any rituals you use, settings or surroundings, postures, texts, etc., and describe your state of mind/heart.

Judith Valente writes about taking seven sacred pauses throughout the day: "Our pauses can be as brief as stopping to observe a bird or a flower bed . . . or as simple as breathing attentively."

Tell how you might incorporate seven sacred pauses throughout your day and how you imagine practicing the seven sacred pauses may affect your daily life.

Brother Paul writes, "I usually spend thirty or forty minutes after Mass in mindful meditation trying to stay present to the moment. This is one of the easiest, as well as hardest practices, because I tend either to fall asleep or get restless. As I have learned from experience, I drift off because I am bored with my own mind. Meditation is not hard, as long as I do what I sat down to do, which is to stay present with the Presence. Then I can stay focused, or empty, or alert, or content with just being there."

If you have ever practiced meditation, describe your biggest struggle with it—describe any external and/or internal obstacles you encounter (like Brother Paul's inner boredom or maybe noisy neighbors interrupting your silence). When you encounter these obstacles, describe your response.

Friendship

Judith Valente writes, "My own sense is that friendship involves a deep and abiding devotion that can transcend frequent separations, geographic distance, and diverse life experiences."

Define your understanding and experience of friendship. Be as detailed as possible, describing your experience of friends you have (and have had) over the years, and how geography and life experiences affected your friendships.

"I think," writes Brother Paul, "the capacity for friendship is elemental to spiritual development, as well as to human maturity. That does not mean that you have to claim a lot of friends; it means that the ability to handle intimacy is essential. . . . You don't have to know everything about another person, or they about you. . . . In fact, friendship can be ruined by too much intimacy."

Describe how your experience of friendship connects with/supports your spiritual development. Also describe how your experience of friendship avoids "too much intimacy," and why that may be a good thing for your relationships.

Brother Paul also writes, "All friendship is good while it lasts, but to cling to a relationship readily spoils it."

Tell about a time when either you or a friend tried to "cling" to your relationship. Be sure to identify what that clinging looked and felt like, and the effect it had on your friendship.

Navigating the Unexpected

"In the open," writes Brother Paul, "is where we start and that is where we go. Or maybe there is no coming and no going, just standing under the sky and being open to what happens moment by moment. . . . What matters is that we try not to explain what happens, that we not ignore it or wish that it were all different. What is, is what it is." In response, Judith Valente writes about receiving an unexpected diagnosis.

Describe a time in your life when you experienced an event that was totally unexpected, something that truly "came out of left field." Tell how you navigated that experience. Describe in detail your response to the unexpected and tell what, if anything, you would change about your response.

Brother Paul writes, "Perhaps life does us a favor when it blindsides us with a crisis. Perhaps it does this just to remind us that we are not in total control. I am not sure that this always brings us an awareness of the *true* self; but it certainly does bring us to the *real* self, with all its limitations."

Describe what you learned about yourself when you experienced a particular crisis, and tell how you apply that lesson learned as you live your post-crisis life.

Meditation

Citing the Buddhist nun Pema Chödrön, Brother Paul writes, ". . . we should not meditate with any expectation that we will eventually get better at it. Likewise, we mustn't expect to become better people or more enlightened people. . . . I'm no better at meditation after sixty-plus years in the monastery, it appears, than I ever was."

Describe any expectations you have of meditation—detail how those expectations may hinder your meditation practice.

Continuing, Brother Paul describes meditation as ". . . a moment to abide with that sense of being on the threshold. . . . That is the moment of mercy, a moment to realize that ultimately, it is not all up to me. I can relax and allow existence to be as it is."

Describe how Brother Paul's experience in meditation compares with your own. It's OK to have a similar or a very different experience—just be as detailed as possible.

Living with the Unimaginable

During the first months of the COVID-19 pandemic, as the country locked down, Judith Valente wrote, "My concept of sacrament is also evolving. As Catholics, we tend to think of sacraments as specific rituals meant to reflect God's grace in the world . . . Now is the time to become sacraments for each other—visible, human signs of God's grace in the world."

Identify and describe a person who has been a sacrament to you during the pandemic. Also tell how you may have been (or tried to be) a sacrament to others.

Brother Paul responds by observing the difficulty some have with prayer during lockdown without access to churches: "I have to say that I often cannot pray *more* effectively at home or in church. But that is the way of prayer for a monk who is getting on in years. The fact that I can do either and both *at all* is a reason for gratitude, and gratitude is the real core of prayer."

Describe what you have learned about gratitude during the pandemic—what/who are you grateful for? How has gratitude informed your prayers? How has your practice of gratitude affected your life during the pandemic?

Useless Care

Judith Valente quotes Thomas Merton's final address as novice director at Gethsemani: ". . . the thing we all seek one way or another . . . is some assurance that it is possible in this kind of [Christian] life 'to put away all care.' This doesn't mean walking around with a dismissive attitude toward everything, however. Rather it's about dispensing with useless care . . ."

Tell how you put away all "useless care." Identify cares you may have that distract you or feed anxiety, as well as tell about how you try to put them away. Be as detailed and descriptive as possible, giving examples.

Brother Paul responds with Merton's observation that "life [is] an opaque package with something inside. We take off the wrapping only to find another layer. We keep taking off layers of wrapping . . . to find that there is *nothing* there. His point isn't that life is an empty void, but that . . . the sacredness of everything is obvious and we are missing it. God is evident all around . . ."

Using as much detail as you can, describe how you experience the "sacredness of everything," and how that experience may seem like nothing at all and/or everything all at once—or something entirely different.

Nature's Magic Spots

Brother Paul describes a "magic" spot in St. Anne's park, "a fairy place" filled with vines and shrubs and birds with their song. Judith Valente responds that one of her "meditation places" is her "screened-in front porch." "We all need a magic spot, or more than one," she writes.

Describe your own "magic spot" or spots, and be sure to tell in detail what makes them magical to you.

Cultivating Silence

"A silent mind brings a silent presence," writes Brother Paul. He tells of being a young monk with the nickname "Grandslam" because he made so much noise in the kitchen in a monastery dedicated to silence. "I punished my own ears with that noise as well, but I have since learned to be easier on myself. Stress creates noise and noise creates stress, all without our knowing it."

It's easy to use noise to distract us from the noise we carry inside our own heads. Describe how you find silence in your life, or how you'd like to.

Judith Valente responds, "Some of the worst intrusions [are] ... from the 'white noise' of texts, email, and social media. My email inbox dings constantly ... Every once in a while, I need to take a break from all the messaging or I feel I will go crazy."

If this "white noise" sounds familiar to you, tell how you plan (or what you already do) to turn down the volume.

Living in Eternity

Judith Valente and Brother Paul close the book with letters that declare their friendship. Brother Paul writes, "I know you and you know me. But wait. I hardly know myself—at least not in the totality of what I will be. The little letters we write, the casual contacts we make in life, the fragments of acquaintance, the relationships broken or made whole are just the beginning. Each is a small seed of what can develop in eternity. None of it is lost. Nothing is ever lost." "That is how I feel about our exchanges," Valente responds, "that through them I have somehow been experiencing a small taste of eternity."

Describe where, and/or with whom, you have experienced "a small taste of eternity" where "nothing is ever lost."

ABOUT THE AUTHORS

JUDITH VALENTE is a former staff writer for the *Washington Post* and the *Wall Street Journal* and a finalist for the Pulitzer Prize in journalism. Valente contributes to *US Catholic* magazine and *National Catholic Reporter*. She is the author of *How to Live*. Learn more at *www.judithvalente.com*.

BROTHER PAUL QUENON, OCSO, entered the Trappist Abbey of Gethsemani in 1958 at the age of seventeen. He is the author of the memoir *In Praise of the Useless Life* and several books of poetry. Thomas Merton was his novice master and spiritual director.

Hampton Roads Publishing Company

... for the evolving human spirit

Hampton Roads Publishing Company publishes books on a variety of subjects, including spirituality, health, and other related topics.

For a copy of our latest trade catalog, call (978) 465-0504 or visit our distributor's website at *www.redwheelweiser.com*. You can also sign up for our newsletter and special offers by going to *www.redwheelweiser.com/newsletter/*.